QUICKSILVER

QUICKSILVER

The Ted Binion Murder Case

Photographs by Jeff Scheid
Text by John L. Smith

Huntington Press
Las Vegas, Nevada

Quicksilver: The Ted Binion Murder Case

Published by
    Huntington Press
    3687 South Procyon Ave.
    Las Vegas, Nevada 89103
    (702) 252-0655 Phone
    (702) 252-0675 Fax
    e-mail: books@huntingtonpress.com

ISBN 0-929712-28-5

Cover Design: Bethany Coffey Rihel
Interior Design: Laurie Shaw
Production: Laurie Shaw

Photos: Jeff Scheid
Text: John L. Smith

Additional Photo Credits: Tom Dillard pg. 18; Craig Moran pg. 19;
Clint Karlsen pgs. 23, 24, 164, 165; John Gurzinski pg. 151; Jim
Laurie pgs. 151, 152

Printing History
1st Edition—2001

For the staff and management of the
Glendive Ranger-Review *and the*
Las Vegas Review-Journal *for believing in me.*

—*Jeff Scheid*

For Harry, Ralph, and all the members of
Benny Binion's Horseshoe Club roundtable,
men who kept the secrets of the old Las Vegas.

—*John L. Smith*

Acknowledgments

Although writing and photography are solitary pursuits, daily journalism and book publishing are team efforts. We're fortunate to be members of an excellent team of writers, photographers, editors, managers, and legal advisers at the *Las Vegas Review-Journal*. We would like to thank the following people from the *Review-Journal* for their support and professionalism: Publisher Sherman Frederick, General Manager Allan Fleming, and Editor Tom Mitchell for spearheading the collaboration with Huntington Press. Also Steve Andrascik, Warren Bates, Amy Beth Bennett, Pamela Busse, Kevin Cannon, Norm Clarke, Glenn Cook, James Decker, Ralph Fountain, Carri Geer, John Gurzinski, Don Ham, Mark Hinueber, Mary Hynes, Clint Karlsen, Jim Laurie, Craig Moran, Jane Ann Morrison, Padmino Pai, Trudy Patterson, Natalie Patton, Glenn Puit, David Stroud, Gary Thompson, Christine Wetzel, Ched Whitney, Charles Zobell, and former *R-J* reporters Ben Rogers, Joe Schoenemann, and Mike Zapler. A special thanks to *Review-Journal* court reporter Peter O'Connell, whose trial coverage was consummately professional. Thanks especially to Huntington Press' Deke Castleman, Anthony Curtis, Bethany Rihel, and Laurie Shaw.

The generosity and insight of private investigator Tom Dillard, whose unique view of the Binion murder case is the subject of a separate book, was invaluable. He also provided us with photographs of the Binion vault in Pahrump. We owe you one, Tom.

We would also like to thank District Judge Joseph Bonaventure, court clerk Al Lasso, District Attorney Stewart Bell, Chief Deputy District Attorneys David Roger and David Wall, Binion estate attorneys Richard Wright and Harry Claiborne, as well as defense attorneys Louis Palazzo, John Momot, Bill Terry, Robert Murdock, Tom Pitaro, and Steve Wolfson, and Clark County public-information specialist Doug Bradford and his staff. District Court Administrator Chuck Short and his staff provided valuable assistance. Bailiffs Matt Diamond and Hank Pyla were also helpful.

As ever, thanks to Jenny Scheid, Tricia Smith, and Amelia Smith for their encouragement, patience, and understanding.

Contents

The Properties of Quicksilver

Las Vegas has always been a good place for murder. The intoxicating mixture of gambling, sex, and booze can make for a lethal cocktail for anyone who overindulges in the city's celebrated traditions. Add drugs to the potion, and the outcome is all but assured. Around these parts, often all that separates high society and the lowlife subculture is the size of one's bankroll. And there's always someone willing to try to separate a man from his money.

The September 17, 1998, death of high-living casino man Ted Binion swept across the Las Vegas valley like a late-summer thunderstorm delivering a 100-year flood. The facts of the case were played out like so much sensational thunder and lightning in the media. From the first suspicion that Binion's drug overdose might not have been accidental to the sentencing of his live-in lover, Sandra Renee Murphy, and his one-time friend, Montana contractor Richard Bennett Tabish, the case cast a spell over followers of true-crime courtroom drama across the country.

What made the Binion murder special?

Several things. First, the facts surrounding the death itself were in such dispute that for months expert investigators and medical examiners differed on whether he had died of an accidental drug overdose or something more sinister. And there was the specter of the Binion family, a legendary Las Vegas casino clan known as much for its tumultuous private life as its downtown Binion's Horseshoe gambling hall was known for high-stakes poker games.

Beyond the facts of the case and the timeliness of the death so close to the turn of the century, the Ted Binion story marked the first time in Las Vegas history that a local homicide sustained the interest of the nation. It was the city's first made-for-TV murder.

For many years, the murders most associated with Las Vegas occurred miles from the city. Although Benjamin "Bugsy" Siegel's name had become synonymous with Las Vegas, the gangster developer of the Fabulous Flamingo was murdered in June 1947 in Beverly Hills. When the mob decided in August 1976 to eliminate its longtime Las Vegas lieutenant Johnny Rosselli, the body of the dapper wiseguy was discovered in an oil drum afloat in Dumfoundling Bay off Miami. And while Chicago Outfit enforcer Anthony Spilotro's turf was the Las Vegas Strip, the tough guy and his brother, Michael, were murdered in June 1986 and buried in a shallow grave in an Indiana cornfield.

To be sure, Las Vegas has had more than its share of intriguing murders. There was the 1977 contract killing of union organizer Al Bramlet and the unsolved 1972 car-bombing of FBI agent-turned-casino landlord William Coulthard. The 1974 stabbing death of elderly Hilda Krause rocked the community after her husband's girlfriend, casino cocktail waitress Rosalie Maxwell, and her boyfriend Frank LaPena were implicated in the crime. These love-triangles-turned-deadly, set against the backdrop of the Las Vegas casino nightlife, were irresistible to locals. But in the generation before cable television and "Court TV," few people outside Southern Nevada took notice.

The greatest difference in the Binion case came as a result of changes in the media and the national obsession with true-life drama—the more sordid the better. In 1994, Americans were repulsed yet riveted by the facts and events surrounding the grisly slayings of Nicole Brown Simpson and Ronald Goldman. The O.J. Simpson murder trial, which ended in acquittal in October 1995, changed media trial coverage forever.

While the Binion case did not rise to that dizzying level of attention, it was the Las Vegas community's first nationally televised "trial of the century." Although reporters from major newspapers and national magazines followed the case, "Court TV" made the greatest difference. Its producers positioned two cameras in the courtroom of District Judge Joseph Bonaventure and conducted gavel-to-gavel coverage that included daily interviews with the major players in the case. By night, Geraldo Rivera made the Binion trial a cause célèbre, slanting so heavily in favor of the defendants that he single-handedly turned defense attorneys John Momot and Louis Palazzo into household names, if only for a few short weeks.

The Binion murder case was the subject of controversial daily public opinion telephone polls, advertisements for which were broadcast during breaks in the television coverage of the trial. The results of those polls, which showed overwhelmingly that the public had prejudged the defendants and convicted them of murder long before the jury did, became such a contentious issue that Judge Bonaventure was forced to call a hearing to discuss the matter. The polls were discontinued, but not before their results were broadcast on national television.

Never before in Las Vegas history had a court case been so scrutinized and so awash in media. In a city built on sin, entertainment, and hyperbole, it was the ultimate form of theater.

In my opinion, no photojournalist captured the courtroom drama and the greater spectacle surrounding the Binion trial than award-winning *Las Vegas Review-Journal* photographer Jeff Scheid. The Montana native and devoted Las Vegas amateur historian had not only chronicled the Binions for many years, but was present from the first pretrial motions through the sentencing of Murphy and Tabish to life in prison. He took hundreds of pictures of the key players and their families, but due to the newspaper's space limitations, only a few dozen were published during the trial. His photographs provide an accurate and compelling window through which future generations will be able to get a dramatic sense of an important turning point in Las Vegas history. As you'll see, with his camera Jeff Scheid is one helluva reporter.

For my part, I wrote dozens of columns about aspects of the case, and it was only after months of skepticism and research that I came to the conclusion that my acquaintance, Ted Binion, had been the victim of murder and not his life's own dangerous excesses. In a case in which some representatives of the media decided that a murder had been committed long before the first facts had been gathered, it's important to note that the Binion affair was at no time a neat package of a homicide. The elements that made it so messy and circumstantial—and so irresistible—are some of the issues that the defendants are using to appeal their murder convictions. I have attempted to give readers a concise narrative of the case, which contained so many dark elements of the real Las Vegas Story.

More than the title's double-entendre, the Ted Binion murder case possessed many of the properties of quicksilver, or mercury as it is more commonly known. This, in words and pictures, is the true tale of a fast fortune that was impossible to hold and, ultimately, poisonous to the touch.

John L. Smith
January 2001

QUICKSILVER
The Ted Binion Murder Case

Ted Binion's voice on the phone was as animated as ever. From inside my cramped office at the *Las Vegas Review-Journal*, I straightened up and listened closely. A conversation with the hard-living, hedonistic, casino-cowboy son of Las Vegas legend Benny Binion promised to be anything but boring.

It was Tuesday, September 15, 1998.

In a cigarette-scarred Texas drawl undiminished by a lifetime mostly in Las Vegas, Binion asked whether I might be interested in collaborating with him on a book about his family, as well as a fast-action film-script idea he had in mind. He knew that I was fascinated by his family's place in Las Vegas history. In the time that we'd known each other, we'd talked intensely about the old Las Vegas, and I had come to believe that the past was the place Ted Binion felt most comfortable.

Binion had abused his body and spirit for years with drugs, alcohol, and fast women. It was well known in gambling and law-enforcement circles that he had a weakness for black-tar heroin and hard-bodied young women. A man with his bankroll and connections could find a lifetime supply of both in Las Vegas. Heroin addiction had not only ruined his marriage and other relationships, but was a contributing factor in the revocation of his privileged Nevada gaming license. Lonnie Ted Binion, the Nevada Gaming Commission had unanimously decided earlier in the year, was too wild for the corporate casino culture of Las Vegas. Despite all his juice, he was unlikely ever again to work at the casino his father had made

Ted Binion

Binion's Horseshoe Casino

famous, Binion's Horseshoe Club, on Fremont Street downtown.

While most of our conversations concerned the past, this time Ted surprised me by talking about the future. He was thinking of selling his Pahrump ranch and buying a bigger spread in Northern California or Southern Oregon. With a personal net worth rumored to be as much as $100 million, he could afford to write a check for whatever slice of paradise he desired.

We agreed to get together soon to talk about his ideas. Although I liked the thought of a Binion family history, his movie was even more intriguing. It was about the son of a casino man, a cross-country trip, drugs, and the mob. He had it all worked out in his head, he said, and just needed someone to help him get it down on paper.

Two days later, Ted Binion was dead of an apparent drug overdose at his home at 2408 Palomino Lane. He was 55. Like a lot of Las Vegans, I assumed he'd gone the way of most aging junkies. But like a lot of Las Vegans, I was wrong. The story of Ted Binion's death was even more gripping than any tale told about him in life.

◊ ◊ ◊

To understand the Binion family's place in Las Vegas history, it's necessary first to know something about its patriarch. Lester Ben Binion was born in Pilot Grove, Texas, in 1904. The Binion clan farmed a little and raised some cattle, but it was horse trading that captured the young boy the family called Benny. He started gambling as a teenager and by his early 20s was running his own games. By the time of the Great Depression, Benny Binion was on his way to vying for the lucrative but dangerous status of king of the Dallas racket bosses.

An integral part of any racketeer's success is his ability to get along with the local police and political machine, and for years Benny greased the wheels with the best in the business. Accused of three murders and suspected of several others, Binion also enjoyed uncommon good luck. But by the end of World War II, he was beset by a reform movement in the sheriff's office and a few too many enemies.

Benny Binion

The Binion family circa 1955. L-R Clockwise: Benny, Jack, Ted, Becky, Brenda, Teddy Jane, Barbara; Barbara's son, Key Fechser, is seated on lap.

In 1946, Benny moved his family from Dallas, where gambling was illegal and likely to get a man killed, to Las Vegas, where gambling was legal and the mob maintained the peace. As the story goes, Benny made the trip across the desert in a Cadillac loaded down with $2 million in cash. He resettled his family, which eventually included his wife Teddy Jane, sons Jack and Ted, and daughters Barbara, Brenda, and Becky.

In Las Vegas, Benny Binion worked at the El Cortez on Fremont Street before buying the Westerner Club and the Apache Hotel, which was later transformed into

Above: Teddy Jane Binion in the cage during the 1985 World Series of Poker.

Right: from l-r, Jack, Teddy Jane, and Ted at Teddy Jane's birthday party in 1992.

Binion's Horseshoe Club. Under Benny's influence, the Horseshoe gained a reputation far and wide as an unpretentious gambling hall where the house would fade a player's largest bet. But an income-tax-evasion conviction made Binion too controversial for Nevada's fledgling system of gaming regulation, so he quickly groomed his sons Jack and Ted to run the casino, with the chain-smoking Teddy Jane in the count room. The Horseshoe Club never missed a beat. After serving out his time on the federal tax bit, in his capacity as Director of Publicity, Benny held court for a variety of humanity—ranging from wiseguys and gamblers to judges and politicians—every day in the casino coffee shop.

"I'm very well pleased with my family," Benny Binion said in an interview in 1973. "They're all good workers. My wife works here, and my daughter [Barbara]. They count the money and look after the office. Jack is the boss. We get along real good."

Jack Binion was always the responsible son in the family. Ted, on the other hand, idolized his father's racketeer past and gangster associations. Although a skilled casino man possessed of an uncanny ability with figures, Ted Binion struggled. In 1976, he was a suspect in the murder of Rance Blevins, an unruly Horseshoe customer who had made the deadly mistake of busting up the house that Benny built. In 1986, Ted was arrested in a large-scale police investigation into heroin trafficking in Southern Nevada. He eventually pleaded guilty to a misdemeanor, but he lost his state gaming license.

Binion and other Horseshoe employees were indicted in 1990, charged with robbing and beating Horseshoe customers whom they'd accused of cheating or otherwise deemed undesirable. That case was later dismissed. In 1993, when he agreed to pay a fine and undergo random drug testing, Ted Binion's gaming license was reinstated.

Top: Sister Brenda holding Ted; Bottom: Ted as a boy; Above: At the ranch.

For all his personal demons and brushes with the law, Ted Binion appeared to prosper away from Las Vegas, and for a time he operated the family's 160,000-acre ranch in Montana. There, Ted could fish, play cowboy, and steer clear of the bad influences lurking in the shadows of Fremont Street. But he couldn't stay away from Las Vegas forever. Sin City was in his blood, and he itched to return to operate the Horseshoe.

Although he claimed he'd kicked his multimillion-dollar heroin-smoking habit, Metro police and state Gaming Control Board sources

Becky Binion Behnen and Jack Binion battled for control of the Horseshoe in the late '90s

indicated otherwise. He managed to remain in position at the casino, but his home life fell apart. By March 1995, Doris Kilmer Binion had filed for divorce and Ted was a fixture as a free-spending barfly on the late-night topless-cabaret circuit.

What anchors existed in his life were either dead (Benny died in 1989; Teddy Jane in 1994) or had fled. Instead of combining their strengths, the sons and daughters of Benny and Teddy Jane began quarreling over the family fortune and the future of the Horseshoe. Jack and Ted became embroiled in a battle for control of the casino against their youngest sister Becky Behnen and her husband Nick. Jack eventually sold his interest to Becky after a nasty litigation and Ted was forced out after the state Gaming Control Board began investigating his narcotics use and propensity for hanging out with local mob figures.

Then, one night at Cheetah's topless bar on Western Avenue near the Strip, Ted Binion met Sandy Murphy. She was a honey-blonde hard-bodied 23-year-old who had ended up on stage in an effort to make enough cash to pay a $13,000 gambling debt at Caesars Palace. She pulled up a stool next to him at the bar and they began drinking shots of tequila. Although she danced for him, she was

Sandy and Ted became a couple in 1995.

not by profession one of the exotic young gypsies who hustle cash in a G-string and high heels at the club. Nor was she among the legion of Las Vegas women who work as prostitutes. Sandy told Ted she and a girlfriend, Linda Carroll, had been selling lingerie and outfits to some of the dancers.

Ted was attracted to her. He liked the way she could switch from high-school coquette to foul-mouthed biker bitch in a heartbeat. But she knocked him off his feet when she turned down a wad of cash he offered her to help pay her gambling debts. Although his family name was legendary in the gambling world, Murphy claimed not to know who he was, at one point calling him "Ted Bunyan." It was only after he took her to the Horseshoe that she began to see that he wasn't just another sweet-talking drunk in worn blue jeans, but a man of vast wealth.

In short order, Ted and Sandy became an item. In April 1995, she moved into his 6,000-square-foot house on Palomino Lane. Although she insisted that theirs was a typical conjugal relationship, it was clear from her monthly credit-card bills that her definition of normal included days spent buying expensive clothes at tony Strip boutiques and nights at gourmet restaurants. For a girl who liked to say that she came from a normal working-class family in Southern California, she was in reality a party girl who had no difficulty ad-

Sandy, far left, was a notorious party girl.

justing to the high-flying life a relationship with Ted Binion encompassed.

But as the Eagles song goes, every form of refuge has its price. Living with Ted Binion also meant dealing with his drug abuse, paranoia, growing list of enemies, and fits of violence. After one particularly nasty exchange in which Sandy vowed to pack her burgeoning wardrobe and leave him, Ted made amends by buying her a $90,000 Mercedes.

At the time, Ted was being hounded by the pesky agents of the Gaming Control Board and Jack Binion was distancing himself from his younger brother. Ted, in turn, blamed his sister Becky and brother-in-law Nick Behnen for his problems with the casino authorities. Finally, Ted was forced out of the family operation. On his way out, he was suspected of removing several hundred thousand dollars worth of $5,000 chips, which later turned up in the hands of numerous local poker players and long-time Horseshoe customers.

Ted Binion had another problem. When he left the Horseshoe, he had to take with him 48,000 pounds of silver bars and coins that had been stored in a 19th century vault at the casino. An appraiser had estimated the value of the silver at $5 million, but Binion believed his treasure to be worth closer to $7 million. The collection

included hundreds of uncirculated silver dollars from a United States mint that had operated in Carson City from 1870 to 1893. Toting a shotgun, Binion supervised the transfer of the silver from the vault to a temporary storage site: the garage of his Palomino Lane home.

Ted had his enemies, but he also had his old friends. There were his attorneys, former federal Judge Harry Claiborne, Richard Wright, and Jim Brown. One trusted insider was Brad Parry, a surveillance specialist who worked as the caretaker at the Binion family's Bonanza Road ranch house. Most of Binion's other friends had one thing in common, felony status. David Mattsen, for example, was an ex-felon who served as foreman of his Pahrump ranch. Ted admired outlaws and imagined himself to be one. Also, like most drug users, he was distrustful of squares.

Left: Harry Claiborne, Right: Richard Wright, Bottom: Jim Brown

By early 1998, Ted Binion had added a new friend to his circle, a young, handsome, trucking-company owner named Rick Tabish. Like Murphy, Tabish had met Binion by accident at a place he frequented, Piero's restaurant. Tabish, whose wife and children were back home in Missoula, quickly endeared himself to Binion with colorful stories of his reckless Montana youth, business exploits, and felony convictions for drugs and the theft of an expensive oil painting.

Tabish neglected to mention that he was near bankruptcy and

that his dream of getting rich by hauling tons of gravel to be used for construction in booming Southern Nevada had been ruined by Leo Casey, a diminutive character with a reputation as a con man. Tabish had entered into a partnership with Casey and Californian John Joseph. Together, the three planned to make their fortunes in the gravel trade. Casey secured the claims to mine the gravel; he also bought the machinery. Joseph was responsible for removing the gravel and preparing it for sale. Tabish's trucks would haul the gravel to construction sites around the valley. In short order, contract delays and Casey's apparent double billing on six-figure machinery purchases put Tabish in desperate financial straits. Tabish and Joseph forced Casey out of the deal, which appeared to reduce his problems, but Tabish needed money fast or he faced the possibility of losing everything.

Top: Rick Tabish, Center: Leo Casey, Bottom: John Joseph

In spring 1998, Tabish proved helpful to Ted Binion in solving his problem of where to safely store the $7 million in silver he'd been keeping in his garage. Ted decided that his Pahrump property was the safest place, and true to form he envisioned a dramatic underground vault that he could easily keep an eye on with a gun ever at his side. Tabish not only helped arrange to dig the hole, but to build the vault itself. When it came time to set the combination, only Binion and Tabish knew the numbers that would open the door to a fortune in silver bars and coins.

The subterranean silver vault in Pahrump.

Around that time, Ted Binion's heroin use increased, and his relationship with Murphy disintegrated. Their dysfunctional home, built on hedonistic excess, was coming apart, and she'd begun being seen in public with Rick Tabish. Those who knew that Ted was often on the nod and unavailable or unwilling to go bar and restaurant hopping with Murphy understood when she was seen with a variety of his trusted associates. Still, those who saw Murphy and Tabish motoring around Las Vegas in her Mercedes observed that the two young people made a handsome couple.

As the summer of 1998 wore on, Ted Binion was on a precipitous downward spiral. His dream of returning to the Horseshoe and booting out his little sister and her husband was over. Worse, he was

Ted Binion's licensing problems mounted in 1998.

back on the junk that had crippled him for so long. In the middle of all that, he'd begun hearing rumors that his sweet-talking Sandy was running around with the Montanan, Rick Tabish. The arguments between Binion and Murphy grew more frequent and ferocious. By early September, Binion's friend Brad Parry later recalled, Ted had finally made up his mind to break up with Sandy Murphy.

Whatever his intentions, Ted Binion never got the chance to send his girlfriend packing. At 3:55 p.m. on September 17, 1998, a call came in to the 911 emergency operator. In a halting voice, a tearful Sandy Murphy told the operator that Ted Binion was dead.

When paramedics and police arrived, they found the body of Lonnie Ted Binion, dressed in a shirt and underwear, lying face up on a sleeping bag on the den floor. Next to him was an empty bottle of the anti-anxiety sedative Xanax, the drug of choice for a heroin user attempting either to kick his habit or level out his high.

Upon initial observation, it appeared, even to experienced detectives, that Binion had simply died of an overdose—a typical junkie's death.

Sandy Murphy was hysterical. Attending paramedics called an ambulance, which transported her to nearby Valley Hospital for observation. Although her pulse rate jitterbugged up to 122, hospital personnel later noted that her sobbing and cries of anguish sounded faked. At one point, an attending nurse entered Murphy's room and saw her in bed with a sheet over her head mumbling the words "boo hoo." Murphy claimed to be too distraught to grant an interview with Metro detectives who arrived at the hospital a short while later. Rick Tabish, who said he was on his way to the airport for a flight to Montana, returned to the Palomino Lane house after learning of Binion's death on the radio and dropped by the hospital as well. At one point, Tabish asked Binion attor-

Rick Tabish, left, talks with attorney Richard Wright on the day of Ted Binion's death.

19

ney Richard Wright to keep the police away from Sandy because of her emotional devastation. One officer did manage to interview a wailing Murphy for 12 minutes.

"I tried to make him breathe, and he wouldn't breathe," Murphy told the officer.

Metro police Sgt. Jim Young later said, "Preliminary results indicate he may have made an ingestion error in regards to medication."

◊ ◊ ◊

The very next day, Becky Behnen went public with her suspicions that her brother, despite his notorious drug use, may not have died from an overdose. The rest of the family remained silent, partly in stunned amazement that Becky, who'd had a hand in causing Ted so much trouble, was suddenly weeping at his demise. Ted often said how much he hated Nick Behnen, whom he believed held his youngest sister under a

Top: Becky Binion Behnen with photos of a young Ted in the foreground.

Right: Nick Behnen

Svengali-like spell. Behnen, in turn, had made his malevolence toward Ted clear. Both Behnens later scoffed at such sentiments, assuring skeptics that, despite their differences, they shared a mutual respect for one another. When Ted drank or used drugs, they insisted, he was irrational and said things he didn't mean. Among them were death threats against his sister and brother-in-law.

Binion always kept large amounts of cash, from $50,000 to more than $500,000, at his house, as well as coin collections and silver dollars. But after combing the premises, neither police nor estate investigators found the kind of currency the deceased had considered walking-around money. It was missing. Sandy Murphy immediately blamed the Binion clan and its allies, such as estate attorney James Brown, for burglarizing the house. They, in turn, pointed fingers at Murphy.

As executor of his brother's estate, Jack Binion kept his suspicions to himself. He instructed estate attorney James Brown to hire a private investigator to look into Ted Binion's death. Brown later testified about a conversation he claimed to have had with Ted, who told him, "Take Sandy out of the will if she doesn't kill me tonight. If I'm dead, you'll know what happened."

Brown hired former Metro Homicide Bureau detective Tom Dillard, who had spent 23 years with the department and had investigated more than 200 murders. Enlisting Dillard's services proved to be one of the most important decisions anyone would make in a case Metro supervisors were calling an "apparent overdose."

Tom Dillard

◊ ◊ ◊

Less than 48 hours after Binion's death, 60 miles northwest of Las Vegas in Pahrump, Nye County Sheriff's Department deputies were making their rounds. The desert town had been jammed with tourists in for the community's annual Harvest Festival, and the officers had been busy dealing with the usual array of drunken drivers and domestic disputes. Around 2 a.m. on September 19, Sgt. Ed Howard noticed lights coming from fenced property located near Terrible's Casino. The land was owned by Binion.

Their curiosity led to an encounter with fast-talking Rick Tabish, who assured the officers that he was on the property with the approval of its owner. When the cops weren't satisfied with the answers they received, they asked what was in the belly of the large gravel truck Tabish was driving. Tabish told them the truck was empty and banged on the belly's metal wall to illustrate the point. But the cops weren't buying it, and Tabish, suspiciously, began to change his story. He tried explaining to police that not only was he a close friend of Binion's, but he also had the approval of Nye County Sheriff Wade Lieseke to remove the silver from the vault.

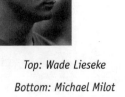

Lieseke was called in. Although the sheriff recalled being contacted by Tabish and Binion ranch foreman David Mattsen, he later denied under oath giving anyone permission to remove the silver from the underground vault. By early morning, the decision was made to charge Tabish, Mattsen, and a man identified as Michael Milot with attempting to steal Binion's 48,000 pounds of silver. Tabish insisted that his close friend Ted Binion had instructed

Top: Wade Lieseke

Bottom: Michael Milot

him, in the event of his untimely demise, to remove the silver from the vault, in order to prevent his family from finding it, and to save it for his daughter Bonnie. Tabish insisted that he had made Sheriff Lieseke well aware that he was bringing a crew out to Pahrump to excavate the site. Why, Tabish claimed, he'd even told attorney Wright he was on his way to Pahrump.

Problem was, Lieseke didn't remember the conversation exactly that way. And Wright didn't recall any conversation with Tabish at all. One Nye County officer later recalled Tabish saying that Binion had wanted to "clean himself out" of the heroin in his system, but had accidentally overdosed.

When it came time for Rick Tabish to post the $100,000 bail set for the Nye County burglary and theft charges, the paperwork was signed by Sandy Murphy.

◊ ◊ ◊

Publicly, Metro Homicide Lieutenant Wayne Petersen remained skeptical that Ted Binion had been murdered. He reminded inquiring reporters that the death scene revealed no apparent signs of foul play. An autopsy showed no conclusive physical evidence of trauma and nothing to indicate violence. A toxicology report would be needed to determine a cause of death.

"There are a few things we're looking into," Petersen told reporters, "but there's still nothing to indicate a homicide."

The empty Xanax bottle, which had been recently filled with 120 tablets, gave rise to speculation that Binion may have committed suicide, a theory family and friends immediately discounted.

Privately, Binion estate investigator Tom Dillard was already interviewing witnesses.

◊ ◊ ◊

Ted Binion's funeral on the afternoon of Tuesday September 22 at Christ the King Catholic Church was loaded with local lawyers, politicians, and judges, as well as casino workers, cowboys, hustlers, wiseguys, and other friends of the family. Already unwelcome around the Binion family, Sandy Murphy arrived at the funeral flanked by her attorneys, legendary mob lawyer Oscar Goodman and his partner David

Top: Ted Binion's boots, hat, and rope were brought to his funeral.

Center: Sandy Murphy attended with her attorney, David Chesnoff.

Bottom: Pallbearers included Michael Gaughan (front right), Richard Wright (front left), and Harry Claiborne (second left).

Chesnoff. Former U.S. District Judge Harry Claiborne, himself an ex-felon after a 1983 tax-evasion conviction, gave the eulogy and described his long-time friend, Ted Binion, as a troubled man with a rare gift for numbers and arguably the best casino mind in the business.

Given the fact that it appeared hard drugs had killed Binion, the decision to play his favorite song, Jim Morrison's disturbingly dissonant "The End," struck many of those present as eerie and haunting. Binion's musical hero Morrison, after all, had died of a heroin overdose.

While family and friends grieved, estate attorneys and PI Tom Dillard attempted to prevent Murphy from staking a claim to the Palomino Lane home and the deceased's personal belongings, which easily could have included a fortune in cash. Dillard set to work lining up interviews with the people in Binion's life. One was estate attorney Jim Brown, who reported the telephone conversation with Binion that had taken place on September 16, the day before he died. Brown reported that Binion had ranted about removing Sandy Murphy as a beneficiary from his will. This contradicted instructions Binion had given Brown a few weeks earlier to add a codicil to the will that gave Murphy the Palomino house, valued at $900,000, as well as $300,000 in cash and the contents of the house, which could have added more than $500,000 to the total. The will named Binion's teenage daughter, Bonnie Binion, as the major beneficiary of an estate with an estimated value of $50 million. It also set aside $500,000 for Brown to litigate any disputes arising from the will.

The first dispute occurred before Binion was even in the ground, when Brown attempted to prevent Murphy from re-entering the Palomino Lane house, at one point telling a police officer at the scene that she was no relation to Binion and not even a Nevada resident.

The second arose a day after the funeral, when Metro police attempted to interview Tabish and Murphy concerning the issues surrounding Ted's death raised by the Binion family. Chesnoff, Murphy's attorney, declined to provide his client. Louis Palazzo, the attorney for Tabish, also declined, adding that any police speculation that the two were somehow romantically linked was nonsense.

Especially if Ted Binion simply died of an accidental overdose.

◊ ◊ ◊

In the days that followed Ted Binion's death, investigators interviewed several people employed by him. Housekeeper Mary Montoya-Gascoigne told police that she received a phone call the morning of Binion's death, in which Sandy Murphy told her that Ted was not to be disturbed that day; she could clean the house the following day. Brad Parry, who in addition to acting as a caretaker of the family's Bonanza Road house doubled as a security and surveillance-camera specialist, noted to police that the video recorder at the Palomino Lane house had earlier been disabled. It was an odd coincidence, Parry thought, considering his friend Ted's obsession with security. Parry had removed the recorder in an effort to repair it. Gardener Tom

Loveday told police that when he arrived at 2408 Palomino Lane a little after 9 a.m. on Sept. 17, he found it strange that the backyard drapes were closed and that Binion's dogs, Princess and Pig, were agitated and scratching at the sliding-glass door. And Don Dibble, a former Metro Homicide detective-turned-private investigator, told police Binion had called on September 16 and asked him to begin tailing Murphy. Dibble never got started.

During the early stage of the investigation, Tom Dillard gathered dozens of taped interviews with witnesses and effectively blazed a trail that police began to follow.

The circumstantial evidence quickly mounted.

For example, when chief engineer Willis John Reiker arrived for

Binion's gardener, Tom Loveday

work the morning of Sept. 17 at Sierra Health Services at 888 South Rancho Road not far from the Palomino Lane house, he was surprised to find his long-time friend Ted Binion waiting for him. Binion, Reiker recalled, was angry. He was talking about getting "rid of the broad and her family."

An hour later, convenience-store clerk Marvin Reed greeted Binion as he came through the door to purchase two packs of Advantage cigarettes. Binion was agitated and "high," in Reed's estimation.

By 9 a.m., gardener Tom Loveday arrived at the Palomino Lane house for his weekly mowing and clipping. Loveday would later recall for Dillard that Murphy's black Mercedes was parked on the east side of the house instead of tucked into its usual space in the garage. No other vehicles were around. Loveday finished his work by 1 p.m. without seeing Mary Montoya-Gascoigne, the Binion maid who usually greeted him.

About the time Loveday arrived to mow the lawn, Montoya received a call at her home. It was Sandy Murphy calling to tell her that "Ted wasn't feeling very well," and to just not come in that day.

At 12:04 p.m., local real estate agent Barbara Brown phoned the Palomino Lane house. She'd been working with Binion for more than a month on the possible purchase of several pieces of real estate. Brown had last spoken to Binion at 9 p.m. the previous evening, when the two agreed to meet for coffee at a nearby Starbucks to discuss a land sale.

Barbara Brown

"Hi Sandy, it's Barbara," she later recalled saying. "Is Ted there?"

"No, Barbara, he's out," Murphy replied.

"Out?"

"He's *out*," Murphy said.

"What's wrong? Are you okay?" Brown asked.

"No," Murphy replied, her voice beginning to break. "Nobody understands what it's been like living with a drug addict. ... And this ... I've got this mess to clean up in the bathroom."

Brown offered to come over and assist her, but Murphy declined the assistance.

At 3 p.m. on the day Ted Binion died, Horseshoe Gaming executive assistant Cathy Rose, who handled Binion's personal accounting, was interrupted during a meeting at the company's Industrial Road office. Sandy Murphy was waiting to speak with her. Rose thought it odd that Murphy took time to drive several miles in order to hand her a $150 check made out to Binion from Richard and Debra Craig, who had received a loan from him. Binion was worth millions, and in the years they'd been together, Murphy had certainly never shown an interest in the day-to-day bookkeeping.

As if that weren't strange enough, Murphy called Rose a short time later, at 3:16 p.m., to ask a seemingly meaningless question about the owner of an Alaskan fishing lodge who had befriended Ted.

Police later determined that Murphy was attempting to create an alibi.

At 3:47 p.m., Murphy received a call on her cell phone from Rick Tabish. The call lasted one minute.

At 3:55 p.m., Murphy reported discovering Binion's body on the floor of the den of the Palomino Lane house.

◊ ◊ ◊

In late September, findings from the toxicology study conducted by the Clark County Coroner's Office were released. It was determined that Binion had lethal levels of both heroin and Xanax in his system at the time of his death. Though authorities again leaned toward their initial determination that Binion had simply overdosed, the Binion family, through Dillard and a team of attorneys, contin-

ued to push for a full-scale murder investigation. Attorneys for Murphy viewed the estate's efforts cynically: A homicide investigation was the Binions' not-so-subtle means of preventing Murphy from receiving what was rightfully hers in accordance with the will.

By early October 1998, the Binion case had caught the attention of the national media. Reporters and producers associated with CNN, ABC News, the *Wall Street Journal*, "Dateline NBC," the *Los Angeles Times, Washington Post*, "Unsolved Mysteries," "Inside Edition," "Hard Copy," and a host of other programs began monitoring developments and asking questions. When the Behnens hired White House political consultant Sig Rogich to coordinate media, it only added to the media feeding frenzy. Bird-dog movie producers from Hollywood started calling reporters for the latest skinny on the case.

There was plenty to report; the story was deepening on several fronts. For homicide investigators, the problem was simple: Their fact-based suspicions established motive and opportunity for, but not the method of, murder. They would be foolish to present a case calling the drug-related death of a notorious heroin junkie a homicide. Not only would the cops be laughed out of District Attorney Stewart Bell's office, but they would only add fuel to the claims that local law enforcement was marching on behalf of the Binion estate. Behind the scenes, attorneys for Murphy and Tabish were spinning an ever-expanding web of just such a conspiracy.

Investigator Tom Dillard, however, was continuing to add to police suspicions. Enlisting the assistance of his former Homicide Bureau partner Bob Leonard, Dillard obtained Murphy's cellular telephone records. The records established a pattern of calls between Murphy and Tabish on the day of Binion's death, with that last call at 3:47 p.m., eight minutes *before* Murphy phoned police to report finding Binion's body. The pattern added one more layer of suspicion to the case, but still failed to establish that Murphy had administered the fatal dose.

It did, however, fit the pattern Binion attorneys were hoping to establish in their efforts to prevent Murphy from getting her share of the estate. On October 20, estate attorney Jim Brown filed an affidavit in District Court stating that Binion had called him September

Jack Binion had suspicions.

16 ordering him to bounce Murphy from his will. But when District Judge Myron Leavitt ruled that the September 16 communication between Brown and Binion was not legally binding, the Palomino Lane house, its contents, and $300,000 in cash were awarded to Murphy. The Binion estate immediately appealed and vowed to file litigation against Murphy.

Jack Binion also filed an affidavit. It read in part, "Based

on the information available to me at this time, Ted believed Murphy was having an affair, and intended to sever his emotional and financial relationship with her. The circumstances surrounding Murphy, Tabish, Milot, and Mattsen make it highly probable that they either converted Ted's property or have knowledge regarding the whereabouts of Ted's property that is missing."

◊ ◊ ◊

Tabish and Murphy, perhaps emboldened by the inability of police to prove that a homicide had occurred, began talking to reporters in an attempt to portray their side of the story. At the same time they declined to speak to police, the two began responding publicly to increasingly negative accounts in the press, portraying them as hustlers with troubled pasts who had been sneaking behind Binion's back at the time of his death. They denied they were romantically involved; both expressed undying loyalty to Ted Binion. They blamed Becky and Nick Behnen and the Binion family, calling them consummately greedy. They were, of course, speaking to reporters against the wishes of their attorneys, setting a pattern of reckless rhetoric that would return to haunt them in the months to come.

◊ ◊ ◊

The New Year, 1999, arrived without an arrest in the suspicious death of Ted Binion. However, a protracted battle was anticipated on several fronts as the resolve of all parties hardened.

On the criminal side, the case was being investigated by Metro Homicide detectives Jim Buczek, Tom Thowsen, and Sgt. Ken Hefner, Michael Karstedt of the District Attorney's office, and private detective Dillard. A grand jury was convened to review evidentiary developments in the case, and Chief Deputy

District Attorney David Roger

Sandy seemed to enjoy the spotlight; pictured here with attorneys Oscar Goodman and David Chesnoff.

District Attorney David J.J. Roger of the Major Violators Unit—who was well known to the police and best friends with Dillard—was brought in to whip the case into shape in preparation for a presentation to the grand jury.

On the civil side, Binion estate attorneys pushed for more documentation, while attorneys Goodman, Chesnoff, and R. Gardner Jolley attempted to dissuade District Judge Michael Cherry from compelling the testimony of Sandy Murphy in the probate matter.

When forced to take the stand February 4 in the probate case before Judge Cherry, Tabish invoked his Fifth Amendment right against self-incrimination 98 times. A week later, Murphy pleaded the Fifth more than 200 times and refused to answer questions aimed at establishing her as a chief suspect in both the theft of a fortune in cash and silver coins at the Palomino Lane house and the death of Ted Binion. During the hearing, 81-year-old Harry Claiborne sparred with Chesnoff and Goodman. Claiborne's visible anger was unsettling in light of his long-time friendships with both men; Goodman had defended him for four years on corruption and tax-evasion charges. It was clear to experienced observers that Binion's death had changed many relationships forever.

During the probate hearing, Tabish and Murphy's facade of innocence had begun to crack for the first time. Still, police appeared no closer to determining if Binion had been a victim of homicide, and if so, how.

Harry Claiborne was convinced there had been foul play. District Attorney Stewart Bell, right, was heading toward the same conclusion.

◊ ◊ ◊

Just after dawn on February 19, 1999, Metro detectives and District Attorney's office prosecutors knocked on the door of Sandy Murphy's ground-floor apartment at 251 South Green Valley Parkway. With reporters and television cameras waiting outside, they presented a search warrant, entered, and found the apartment also occupied by Rick Tabish, further establishing that their relationship was more than just a friendship. At the same time, police searched the office of Tabish's MRT Transportation at 9555 South Las Vegas Boulevard, the suspect's home in Missoula, Montana, silver-suspect David Mattsen's residence in Pahrump, and Binion's 60-acre Pahrump ranch. Police continued to add circumstantial evidence linking Tabish and Murphy romantically in their efforts to discredit the suspects' claim of platonic innocence. All the while the suspects' attorneys attempted to battle the bad press with assurances that what could not be explained away as coincidence could be written off as a conspiracy by the Binions to freeze out Sandy Murphy.

The speculation promptly ceased on March 15, 1999, when Clark County Coroner Ron Flud ruled Binion's death a homicide by forced overdose. It was the first time in memory the coroner had held a press conference, and Flud appeared to revel in the attention. He offered no new medical or forensic evidence during his announcement, but said he'd become convinced that a homicide had been committed after consulting with Metro detectives and estate investigator Dillard.

"There are numerous scenarios," Flud told reporters. "We're not to the point we're going to comment on any of the scenarios."

Although coroners commonly take nonmedical evidence into account when classifying the manner of death, the press conference did nothing to diminish defense contentions that the case was being ramrodded by the Binion estate.

The war of words intensified.

"Now that the coroner has determined it is a homicide, we will be stepping up our efforts to serve justice in a timely manner," an understated David Roger said.

"They have nothing of real substance," Murphy's attorney David Chesnoff countered.

◊ ◊ ◊

Although neither District Attorney Bell nor the prosecutors and defense attorneys involved would admit that they anticipated the arrest of Murphy and Tabish, all indications pointed in that direction as May drew to a close. Oscar Goodman, who had decided to run for mayor of Las Vegas, withdrew from the case. So did David Chesnoff, who had vowed to friends that he would represent Murphy as long as he believed she was innocent, a victim of the Binion estate. Bill Terry took up Murphy's defense. Steve Wolfson became Rick Tabish's lawyer, replacing Louis Palazzo,

David Chesnoff's withdrawal as Murphy's counsel may have reflected his doubts of her innocence. Bill Terry, bottom, took the helm.

David Mattsen

who, like Chesnoff, withdrew suddenly and without explanation.

On June 24, 1999, Sandy Murphy and Rick Tabish were arrested and charged with felony conspiracy and murder charges in the death of Lonnie Ted Binion. They were also charged, along with Michael Milot and David Mattsen, with crimes related to the theft of Binion's Pahrump silver fortune. Tabish, along with Las Vegan Steven Lee Wadkins and California businessman John Bradford Joseph, was also charged with the kidnapping, extortion, and assault of Leo Casey, Tabish's business partner in the sand-and-gravel operation. Conspicuous by its absence from Metro Homicide detective James Buczek's 109-page arrest-warrant affidavit was any physical evidence linking the suspects to Binion's death. If the case ever went to trial, the prosecution would be forced to present largely circumstantial evidence that lacked a tangible murder weapon. But Chief Deputy District Attorney David Roger for the first time revealed the structure of the case against the defendants, in which Casey, the diminutive fast-talking con man with the bad toupee, played a key role.

Tabish and Joseph suspected Casey of busting out the sandpit deal by double billing and skimming, and they decided to do something about it. Accompanied by Wadkins, whose family owned its own gravel company, prosecutors asserted they lured Casey to the sandpit in Jean, Nevada, overpowered him, restrained him with thumbcuffs, and proceeded to extract his confession to bilking the partnership. "While Casey was restrained with thumbcuffs, Wadkins stuck a gun in Casey's mouth and threatened Casey," detective Buczek wrote. "At another point, Wadkins inserted a knife under Casey's fingernails. Tabish repeatedly struck Casey about the face and body with a Yellow Pages phone book."

Not that Casey would make the most credible witness if forced to testify at trial. In an unrelated court matter in which he was being sued by investors in a separate sandpit deal, Casey was in essence called a perjurer by a court-appointed mediator. Previous investors considered Casey little more than a con artist.

In addition, the arrest-warrant affidavit for the first time painted details of the events of the last day of Ted Binion's life. He'd been in high spirits, Las Vegas Mayor Jan Laverty Jones had told police. Jones, then a candidate for Nevada governor, had dropped by Binion's home to pick up a $40,000 campaign contribution.

Housekeeper Mary Montoya-Gascoigne gave police a lengthy list of Binion's coins and other valuables as she remembered them from the previous day. She also noted Murphy's extreme anxiety during their brief phone conversation in which she was told not to come to work.

Jan Laverty Jones

Investigators also took the statement of Deanna Perry, a beautician who had serviced Murphy. Perry recalled overhearing a conversation in which Murphy and her girlfriend, later identified as Linda Carroll, discussed their plans to attend a Las Vegas fund-raising gala. Not only did Murphy say she'd have a new outfit to wear to the soiree, but she'd have a new boyfriend as well. Perry recalled Murphy stating that her current relationship with Binion promised to end with his inevitable drug overdose.

Tanya Cropp, Murphy's friend who, just before Binion's death, had accepted a job as his new appointment secretary, also agreed to cooperate with police. Cropp was with Murphy shortly before, and not long after, Binion's death.

And police had little difficulty locating Binion's heroin connection, long-time drug dealer Pete Sheridan who, without seeking immunity, admitted he'd sold Ted 12 balloons of black tar in exchange for cash and a portion of his Xanax prescription. Sheridan also told police that Tabish and Murphy were with Binion the night before he died.

The affidavit also indicated that police agreed with something

Tom Dillard had surmised from the first time he saw pictures of the crime scene: The body of Ted Binion had been posed. The scene was staged.

In response to the police findings, defense attorneys and the defendants unleashed an assault on the prosecution, Binion family, and media, asserting again that it was all a conspiracy to force Sandy Murphy out of the will. Supporting the allegations of official corruption were the Binions' long ties to the city's top political and judicial officials, in front of whom Sandy Murphy and Rick Tabish, it now appeared likely, would stand trial for the murder of Ted Binion.

◊ ◊ ◊

On July 8, 1999, Justice of the Peace Jennifer Togliatti set Murphy's bail at $300,000 and placed her under house arrest. A monitoring device was attached around Murphy's ankle. A $30,000 bond was posted by a man Murphy had managed to befriend between Binion's death and her arrest on murder charges. Bill Fuller was a wealthy native of Ireland who had met Murphy at the Aristocrat restaurant. Fuller not only posted her bail, but helped finance her defense and set her up in an up-

William Fuller

scale apartment at Las Vegas' Regency Towers. Fuller, a barrel-chested and robust octogenarian with red hair, declined to be interviewed by reporters, saying only that he was well aware of the Binion clan's reputation and believed Murphy was an innocent young woman, wrongly accused.

Due to his felony record and the violent charges against him, Tabish was denied bail.

◊ ◊ ◊

The preliminary hearing in Jennifer Togliatti's court began in August 1999. It was covered by "Court TV," as well as local reporters and several national-magazine writers. The hearing provided the defense with its first long look at the prosecution's witnesses and evidence. It also gave those in attendance a long look at Murphy's legs. Her dire predicament had done nothing to tone down her taste for short skirts and high heels. She appeared almost giddy in court, occasionally flashing a smile for

Judge Jennifer Togliatti

photographers and joking with her attorneys during recess. She went out of her way to make eye contact with the gallery, but grew emotional when attorneys discussed even small details of Ted Binion's death.

The low "probable cause" threshold of evidence made it a certainty that the case would proceed to trial. The preliminary hearing, though, gave the attorneys, the media, and the public an opportunity to watch a dress rehearsal of what was shaping up to be Las Vegas' "Trial of the Century," which would later take place in the courtroom of District Judge Joseph Bonaventure.

One witness for the prosecution was Montana native Kurt Gratzer, who discussed on the stand Tabish's admission of a murder plot against Binion. This witness, who appeared to suffer from serious mental illness in the form of delusions, detailed his childhood friend's plan to separate Binion from his silver by forcing him to overdose on Xanax. Trouble was, Gratzer also admitted he had offered to help kill Binion, testifying that he thought he might get introduced to Binion at his home, take one of the available weapons, and kill him. He even admitted that, as a former member of the military, he was willing to parachute into the millionaire's Pahrump ranch and assassinate him. At one point, Gratzer became so nonresponsive to attorneys' questions that he was ordered by Togliatti to focus on the moment or risk being held in contempt. It was only a test run, but as a witness for the state, Gratzer had failed miserably.

Beautician Deanna Perry fared little better, admitting that she had not come to police with her story of Murphy's beauty-parlor admission until weeks after Binion's death.

Meanwhile, Tanya Cropp, Murphy's friend and Binion's secretary, was criticized for making inconsistent statements. When a police search discovered Cropp in possession of faxes that itemized the valuable silver coins that had turned up missing from Binion's home after his death, her role in the case became clearer. Cropp admitted that Murphy had entrusted her with the list. Following that lead, investigators soon located approximately 100 pounds of silver coins in the possession of Tabish's brother-in-law Dennis Rehbein of Missoula. Rehbein, who had told his story first to District Attorney's Office Investigator Michael Karstedt, was quickly granted immunity in exchange for his testimony. "The trouble Rick was in," Rehbein would later say, "I didn't really want the coins."

But the most critical question in the four-week hearing was raised in the area of forensic pathology, where the state's two experts appeared to disagree on the cause of death. Chief Medical Examiner Lary Simms, who had performed the autopsy and prepared the toxicology report, testified that Binion had died from lethal amounts of heroin and Xanax. Renowned forensic pathologist Michael Baden, brought into the case by Dillard and the Binion estate, countered that Binion had not ingested enough narcotics to kill himself, but was suffocated.

Forensic pathologist Michael Baden, left, and Chief Medical Examiner Lary Simms had different opinions about the cause of death.

When asked why Binion's body showed so little signs of trauma, Baden coolly remarked that the deceased had been suffocated by a means known as "Burkeing." In such cases, the victim's lungs are so severely constricted that he ceases breathing. Tiny blood vessels behind Binion's eyelids showed signs of rupture, and his face and wrists revealed slight but telltale marks of struggle.

As expected, Judge Togliatti ruled there was enough evidence to proceed to trial. The defendants again changed attorneys. Louis Palazzo returned to represent Tabish and John Momot picked up Murphy's case. In the immediate aftermath of the preliminary hearing, the posturing continued.

Attorney John Momot

Tabish's wife Mary Jo quickly blamed the press for sensationalizing the case and helping to railroad her husband. Her husband, meanwhile, was busy attempting to assist in his own defense by enlisting his friend, Jason Frazer, to contact potential alibi witnesses. It was revealed later that, from his jail cell, Tabish had been trying to find allies who were willing to lie on his behalf. His actions were damaging—each time Tabish opened his mouth or made a move, it seemed, the odds against him increased.

Murphy found a sympathetic ear in veteran TV newsman George Knapp, and in early February 2000 she poured out her heart in a carefully stage-managed interview for which she wore a modest dress with her hair conservatively styled. With attorney Momot at her side, Murphy protested that she had loved and taken care of Binion when few others would. And, despite her short stint on stage at Cheetah's and lavish lifestyle with Binion, she was not the gold-digging bimbo that she'd been portrayed to be by the press.

"Everyone tries to paint me in a really negative light because it's the media and the people that are the driving force behind what's going on. But you know, I'm just an everyday person like everyone else," Murphy told Knapp. "You know I grew up in an upper-middle-class family. I was a normal kid. I liked to do all the things that regular everyday kids like to do."

◊ ◊ ◊

In the weeks leading up to trial, the defense attempted to soften public sentiment against Murphy and Tabish. In pretrial hearings, Momot painted the picture of Murphy as a kind, loving, and committed girlfriend who was the only emotionally stable person in Binion's drug-ravaged life. He also raised the specter of the Binion family's influence, and for the first of many times referred to that influence as the "Binion money machine."

"You have a guy who's a heroin addict, a multimillionaire," Momot told the court. "If he was a porter at the Horseshoe Club instead of a famous guy, I don't think we would be here today. Obviously there were a lot of enablers who surrounded him … and I'm not talking about Sandy Murphy."

The remake of Rick Tabish was rendered more complicated by his incarceration in the Clark County Detention Center and his astounding inability to refrain from meddling with potential alibi witnesses. In his spare time, he placed calls to local reporters, making cryptic statements and unsubstantiated allegations against prosecutors and the Binion family. In addition, Tabish was visited in jail by Salvatore "Sammy" Galioto, a Chicago mob associate and the son of an Outfit underboss. Galioto's sudden appearance in a case with so many once-removed mob connections could have opened the door for the defense to present an alternative theory.

Attorney Louis Palazzo

But attorneys Momot and Palazzo were unwilling to pursue the organized-crime angle, and instead offered rampant drug abuse, ultimately leading to suicide, as the cause of Binion's demise. The argument appeared to hold some merit, for Binion had lost his gaming license, was in the process of losing his three-year live-in girlfriend, and appeared to have lost the latest skirmish in his long battle with heroin addiction at the time of his death.

But suicide was easily countered by witnesses who had spoken to Binion in the days and hours before his death. One after another noted that he was making plans for the future and was even willing to place a long-shot $40,000 bet that Jan Jones would win the governor's race, which might somehow help him regain his lost casino license.

Just days before trial, attorney Oscar Goodman was approached by Murphy benefactor Bill Fuller in an attempt to get him to join the defense team. Although rumors were rampant of his participation through trial consultant and close

William Cassidy

associate William Cassidy, the future Las Vegas mayor declined an offer that was estimated at $1 million. He also denied the published reports that attempted to link him with the defense via a deeply covert consultancy.

"I was approached and received an offer, but I turned it down," Goodman said later. "I was running for mayor and had decided not to take on any new clients."

Goodman, whose friend Cassidy was not only consulting for the defense but helping to generate public-opinion surveys on the case through a partnership with advertising man Tom Letizia and political consultant Jim Ferrence, also recognized that no one who participated in the Binion case would come away unscathed in the public eye.

◊ ◊ ◊

The murder trial of Sandra Renee Murphy and Richard Bennett Tabish began March 27, 2000, with jury selection in the packed courtroom of District Judge Joseph Bonaventure. Transfixed by the ordeal they were watching and the ugly revelations they were hearing, the parents and family members of both defendants sat quietly in the gallery. A section was chained off for reporters, and "Court TV" had two cameras covering the action. The courtroom was so crowded in the trial's first few days that members of the public had to stand in line to obtain one of the few passes available to nonfamily.

The blunt Bonaventure steadily moved the attorneys through the voir-dire jury-selection process. Although the case had been covered daily in the city's newspapers and nightly on local television, and defense-sponsored opinion polls conducted by Magellan Research revealed that most Southern Nevadans knew something about the case and believed the defendants were guilty of the crimes alleged, a jury was seated in just three days after 100 interviews. If the polls were accurate, several of those jurors were lying when they said they had no knowledge of the Binion case.

The defense spared little expense for the all-important empaneling process. They hired renowned jury specialist Robert Hirshhorn to ensure that the most sympathetic jurors possible were selected.

Although David Roger and his partner, Chief Deputy District Attorney David Wall, had originally planned to call up to 276 witnesses at trial, they trimmed their list to 130 as the jury was seated.

Roger began his opening statement in a halting style that belied the immense work he had poured into the case. He wasn't flashy, and his stammer was initially distracting, but jurors listened closely to what he had to say.

"Ted Binion was mur-

Judge Joseph Bonaventure

dered," Roger said. "He was murdered for lust. He was murdered for greed. He was murdered by someone he trusted and her new companion.

Deputy DA David Wall

"… We're not about to paint a picture of a saint. However, he *was* a human being."

In what would be his strongest moment in the entire trial, John Momot in his opening statement called the defendants victims of the Binion money machine, which had conspired to push Sandy Murphy out of Ted Binion's will.

"This case is not about homicide," Momot said. "This case is about heroin. What is so odd about Ted Binion is that he lived so long."

The prosecution began calling its witnesses. Ted Binion was crippled by heroin addiction, agreed his ex-wife Doris Kilmer Binion, who tearfully admitted her ex-husband was prone to acts of spousal abuse. Her testimony was presented early in the prosecution's case in an effort to soften its impact, for Roger and Wall well realized Ted Binion's lifestyle made him an unsympathetic corpse.

Kilmer met Binion in 1965 and moved in with him a short time later. He used marijuana regularly in their early years together, but by 1980 he had graduated to smoking Mexican heroin in a method known as "chasing the dragon."

By the time the couple and their young daughter, Bonnie, had moved into the 5,000-square-foot house at 2408 Palomino Lane, Binion's addiction had caused him to be physically abusive. At one point he even threatened suicide. Kilmer tried leaving, but always returned until their final separation and eventual divorce in the spring of 1995. On the day she left the Palomino Lane house for the last time, she eavesdropped on a conversation and overheard her husband making a date with Sandy Murphy.

Kilmer's testimony gave insight into the habits of a man she knew better than anyone. He stockpiled silver and cash, carried a gun even while in the house, and was haunted by his addiction. In all their time together, she had never known him to lie on the floor for any reason.

"He had silver dollars, and a collection of silver, and just tons of silver at the house," she said. "He enjoyed collecting everything like that. He had an antique money collection, a fairly extensive one, and gold coins of all types. ... At any given moment, $50,000 would probably be a small amount (of cash on hand at home). ... He did have one large amount in his motor boat of about $250,000. He liked to deal in cash."

Then it was Kurt Gratzer's turn.

The cockeyed former serviceman who'd been granted immunity from prosecution in exchange for his cooperation managed to tell his story of how Tabish had confided to him that he was going to kill a Las Vegas casino mogul whose girlfriend he'd been having sex with. His testimony lacked the constant digressions and meandering of his statements given during the preliminary hearing, and to many observers' surprise, defense attorneys Momot and Palazzo were unable to force Gratzer to bolt from the courtroom in panic.

Kurt Gratzer

"He wanted to utilize my services in helping him kill this man," Gratzer told the court. The pair, he said, had discussed various methods of getting the job done, from a straightforward shooting to forcing Binion to ingest heroin and Xanax. Although the witness at times appeared scatterbrained, he managed to hold up under the pressure.

Over the next week, prosecutors Roger and Wall bolstered Gratzer's testimony with witnesses Mike Barger, Jon Berman, Tim Boileau, and Terry Sweeney, all of whom testified that Gratzer had mentioned the Tabish conversation around the time of Binion's death.

Berman, a Missoula pharmacist, testified that Gratzer had contacted him in 1998 to ask about the lethal dosage of two drugs, though he couldn't recall which.

Gratzer had held up on the witness stand, but two days later he was arrested on domestic-violence charges at the Sahara after hotel security guards were called to break up a dispute with his girlfriend, Stacy Otto.

A police search of the Palomino Lane house after Binion's death turned up only a small amount of silver and cash. But all Binion's money couldn't save his marriage, and near the end Kilmer told the court she feared for her life.

Bonnie Binion

Binion's daughter, 19-year-old Bonnie Binion, proved to be one of the prosecution's most compelling witnesses. In a soft voice, she wept as she told the court she loved her father despite his faults. She described Sandy Murphy as a greedy possessive person who sought to isolate and control her father.

"She no longer wanted me to return to the house," Bonnie Binion said. "She threatened to kill both of us."

But the final blow came in June 1998, when the daughter attempted to see her father.

"My father came out of the house and he got in the car and Miss Murphy came outside, and she was screaming and yelling at him and me. She didn't want me on her property and that she would call the police if I didn't leave. ... She called me a bitch."

On September 3, 1998, while at college in Colorado, Bonnie talked long distance to her dad.

"He said Colorado was great for fishing and camping and that he wanted to come up," she testified.

It was the last time Bonnie Binion spoke to her father.

Then came time for beautician Deanna Perry to tell her story of the visit of Sandy Murphy and Linda Carroll to the manicurist office. Like Gratzer, Perry managed to hold up on the stand and emerged from cross-examination unscathed. Perry's testimony was also bolstered by corroborating witnesses.

When 64-year-old Leo Casey was called up to testify, he described the brutal beating he took at the hands of Tabish and Steven Wadkins at the Jean sandpit. When it came time to cross-examine the witness, Palazzo roared into action, picking up a copy of the six-inch-thick Southern Nevada Yellow Pages to demonstrate how unlikely it was that Casey would have been able to endure a beating by the muscular Tabish without suffering so much as a bruise or black eye.

Meanwhile, Sandy Murphy's behavior on September 17 returned to haunt her in open court.

Valley Hospital nurse Larry Krev observed Murphy just two hours after she reported finding Binion's body. "Boy, a little overdramatic, eh?" he recalled telling a police officer at the hospital.

Palazzo, left, didn't buy Casey's phone-book-beating story.

Other witnesses, including Murphy's acquaintance Janice Tanno, at whose house she stayed the night of Binion's death, remembered the supposedly distraught girlfriend asking questions about her place in the will. Tanno testified that Murphy wondered aloud that night whether she would inherit the house.

A videotape shot by Murphy and her attorney at the time, William Knudson, the day after Binion's death was played for jurors and revealed a somewhat less than grieving Sandy. Instead of weeping and wailing, she cursed the Binion family, accusing them and their attorneys of stealing the contents of the home, which she believed

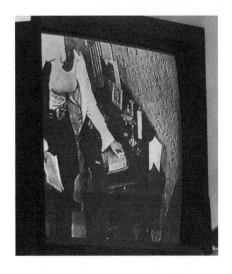

were rightfully hers. The videotape appeared to have a profound effect on the jury, which was able to see for the first time the greedy venal Murphy prosecutors had been attempting to describe.

Then Montana resident Jason Frazer took the stand. Tabish's old friend described how the murder defendant had hired him to generate witnesses who would corroborate his alibi on September 17. Other witnesses would be paid to sully the reputation of private investigator Tom Dillard, whom Tabish believed was behind so much of his trouble. "My life is on the line," Tabish had written his friend. "We need to fight fire with fire."

But Tabish's scheme had backfired. And the jury was left to ask a damning question: Would an innocent person attempt to manipulate and even buy the testimony of witnesses?

Murphy's former friend, Tanya Cropp, testified that the defendant had asked her to conceal a handwritten list of valuable coins. And Tabish's brother-in-law, Dennis Rehbein, testified that Tabish had attempted to sell him some coins after Binion's death. The coins were never recovered.

Sergeant Ed Howard of the Nye County Sheriff's Office told

Jason Frazer

the court that on September 19, while arresting Tabish for burglarizing Binion's Pahrump vault, the defendant told him he was present at Binion's house the day he died, and that Binion had wanted to cleanse himself of heroin by using Xanax. Howard had also caught Tabish in a bald-faced lie when he claimed that the enormous belly-loading gravel truck he was driving was empty. When Howard began to check more closely, Tabish said, "Okay, I lied."

Heroin dealer Peter Sheridan, who did not receive immunity in exchange for his cooperation, testified that he'd not only had a long-standing business relationship with Binion, but had sold him the 12 balloons of black tar on the evening of September 16. And Dr. Enrique Lacayo, Binion's doctor and next-door neighbor, testified that he'd written a prescription for Xanax for the deceased only a day before. But the doctor also said he'd warned Binion to be careful mixing the two drugs.

The prosecution's medical experts differed on the manner of death, but agreed on the cause: homicide. Clark County Chief Medical Examiner Lary Simms calmly filled his testimony with details of Binion's autopsy and toxicology report. Dr. Michael Baden's opinion differed as to the extent of Binion's heroin and Xanax intoxication, and he remained unshakable in his view that Burkeing (suffocation) had been responsible for Binion's demise.

Dr. Baden quotes from his own book, Unnatural Death.

Under examination by prosecutor Wall, Baden gave what some observers later maintained was the most compelling testimony of the trial. Baden's credentials was as impressive as they were prolific: more than 20,000 autopsies performed, more than 70,000 autopsies supervised. He was an internationally respected expert who over 40 years had published and lectured widely, was considered a foremost authority on heroin overdose death, and had even chaired the forensic pathology board for the United States House of Representatives Select Committe on Assassinations, which had re-examined the facts in the murders of President John F. Kennedy and Dr. Martin Luther King Jr. He also was a superb professional witness.

When Baden spoke, people listened.

He detailed for the jury in layman's terms factual elements essential to the prosecution's case. In his professional opinion, the marks on Binion's chest, face, arm and leg pointed to physical trauma that likely occurred shortly before death. The rupture of tiny blood vessels in the eyes told himthat Binion might have experienced physical pressure in the minute before his death.

Although he agreed that a low-level lethal dose of heroin was in Binion's system, Baden said the method of ingestion was almost never fatal.

Wall: "Taking into account your personal experience and the steps you've taken to remain current in the field, how many heroin overdose deaths are you aware of using the method you've described as 'chasing the dragon?'"

Baden: "It almost doesn't occur. I don't think there's been a single case. If this were death by chasing the dragon, I think it would be the first one in the United States of an acute overdose death. ... There is a brain damage condition associated with chasing the dragon, but not death."

Then how did Ted Binion die?

The courtroom sat transfixed; the jurors were mesmerized.

Baden: "My opinion is he died of asphyxia by suffocation. ... My opinion is he died of some obstruction to his nose and mouth, couldn't breathe in, and pressure on his chest."

The defense brought in veteran lawyer James Shellow and promising young local attorney Rob Murdock specifically for the cross-examination of Simms and Baden. Although they made several substantive points, they were unable to goad either forensic pathologist into softening his stance.

The defense also called upon renowned forensic pathologist Cyril Wecht. Wecht, like Baden, was an experienced hired gun. Both Baden and Wecht had been

Dr. Cyril Wecht, left, was a welcome witness for the defense.

retained by counsel in the O.J. Simpson murder case. Wecht stated clearly that Binion had died of a drug overdose, possibly in an act of suicide, but showed no signs of suffocation. There was no homicide at all, Wecht told the jury.

Perhaps feeling that one physician was not enough to offset the testimony of Baden, the consummate professional witness, the defense attempted to overwhelm the jury with several well-spoken experts. They appeared to generate a mixed reaction from the jury. Dr. Jack Snyder, who blasted Baden for his supposed lack of current knowledge on the subject of the effects of mixing narcotics, seemed to irritate jurors. Dr. Robert Bucklin, a 60-year physician, testified that it was impossible to fix a precise time of death of Binion. Backing off slightly from Wecht's hypothesis that included suicide, Bucklin, with 25,000 autopsies to his credit, testified that it was his opinion the deceased died of a simple self-administered drug overdose. Dr. Ray Rawson, a dentist by profession and veteran State Senator, told the court the marks on Binion's face were not the result of a violent struggle.

Dr. Robert Bucklin examines an enlarged autopsy photo of Ted Binion.

While the defense hoped the conflicting medical testimonies would raise a reasonable doubt in the minds of the jury, courtroom observers later surmised that jurors understood that, while Simms and Baden might have disagreed on the precise cause of death, both prosecution experts were certain that a homicide had been committed.

◊ ◊ ◊

It all made for suspense-filled theater, the kind that would win little-watched local cable Channel 1 the top rating of all TV stations in Southern Nevada for the duration of the trial.

Not long after the trial began, Momot and Palazzo, as well as trial consultant Cassidy, began granting interviews to "Court TV" reporter Mary Jane Stevenson and talk-show host Geraldo Rivera, who had taken up the cause of the defense. Commercials for Cassidy's fledgling company, Trial Consultants of Nevada, began to appear opposite the gavel-to-gavel trial coverage on "Court TV" and Channel 1. Prosecutor Roger called the activity unethical and inappropriate, and the ads were discontinued.

"Court TV" correspondent Mary Jane Stevenson.

Tempers and egos flared when Cassidy was accused of threatening Dillard's life, a controversy that provided yet another side-show to the increasingly circus-like events taking place both inside and outside the courtroom.

"Court TV" officials, meanwhile, were impressed by how well the trial played in cities across the nation. Their futures were on the line, but Tabish and Murphy had become television stars. In death, Ted Binion had become the type of notorious celebrity he had so admired in life. Although Southern Nevada's legion of TV soap-opera fans vigorously complained that the trial coverage was pre-empting their favorite programs, within a few days many of them had been converted to the true-life soap opera playing out at District Court.

◊ ◊ ◊

In the end, Roger and Wall trimmed their witness list to 93 and submitted 386 exhibits. They called neither Metro's homicide detectives nor private investigator Tom Dillard. Momot and Palazzo called just 23 witnesses and submitted 167 exhibits.

Defense camp insiders had whispered for weeks that at trial, Momot and Palazzo would do their best to tear apart the Metro detectives who had failed initially to call the death a homicide, and Dillard, whom they considered the point man of the "Binion money machine." Instead, neither Det. James Buczek nor Dillard were called to the witness stand. After Momot's powerful opening statement, all talk of the Binion money machine abruptly ceased. The theory that a rich Las Vegas family had somehow managed to conspire with every player in the Southern Nevada justice system to corrupt the case against the defendants simply faded away.

Instead, the defense chose to focus on suicide as the probable cause of Ted Binion's death. The problem was, the many people who'd seen him in the days leading up to his death painted the picture of a man who was looking forward to moving on with his life, not ending it. The defense had made a critical mistake in calling Binion's death a suicide.

Palazzo caused a stir when he repeatedly asked the judge for permission to smack Tabish with the Yellow Pages. Bonaventure cracked, "This is a new one on me, Mr. Palazzo. You want to beat the hell out of your client?" Bonaventure denied the request, which might have graphically illustrated that Casey was being less than forthright in his testimony. Instead, Palazzo's request drew laughter and derision from courtroom observers. Although Casey's version of events seemed incredible, prosecutors again were able to produce witnesses who appeared to corroborate details of his story.

The nine-woman three-man jury began deliberating on May 10, six and a half weeks after the trial began. When the visibly tired group of jurors filed back into Bonaventure's packed courtroom on May 19 after nearly 70 hours of deliberation, four female jurors were wearing dark glasses. Fore-man Arthur Spear, a retired aerospace-com-pany employee and seven-year Las Vegas resi-dent, read the verdicts:

Richard Bennett Tabish and Sandra Re-nee Murphy were guilty on all counts.

Murphy and Tabish listen to the reading of the verdicts.

Spear's deep voice permeated the courtroom as he read verdict after verdict.

◊ ◊ ◊

"This young lady is strong," Momot told reporters amid the weeping, cheering, and general chaos that followed the reading of the verdicts. "She is going to continue to fight until she is vindi-cated. … She cannot languish in prison for the rest of her life based on evidence that does not show a homicide."

Palazzo, clearly emotionally drained by the verdict, added of his client Tabish, "He should not have been convicted."

Meanwhile, members of the Binion family were celebrating their victory.

"I wanted to be here to show support for Ted," Binion family nephew Bobby Fechser said. "Bill Fuller should have taken that money and shot dice at the Horseshoe."

Meanwhile, at the Horseshoe, Becky Behnen sipped a margarita and answered a reporter's questions. What would Ted say about the verdict?

"He'd be saying, 'The bitch got what she deserved. She's the most evil, devious, deceptive person I've ever met.'"

◊ ◊ ◊

Following the verdict, jury foreman Arthur Spear was criticized for distributing a timeline to his fellow jurors during deliberations that included the phrase "depraved indifference," a term not used by Bonaventure in his jury instructions. One juror, Jane Sanders, later told the court that Spear's actions were inappropriate, while other jurors criticized Sanders for allegedly failing to disclose the fact that some of her family members had been employed by the Binion family. In her affidavit filed on behalf of the defense, Sanders said that, although she voted to convict, she no longer believed Murphy and Tabish were guilty and denied any ties to the Binions or the Horseshoe.

During the penalty phase, defense attorneys and prosecutors argued over the appropriate punishment for the defendants. Although the prosecution had decided months earlier not to seek the death penalty, Roger and Wall vigorously advocated a sentence of life without the possibility of parole. Momot and Palazzo, meanwhile, called on several Tabish and Murphy family members to testify. Predictably, they all painted pictures of the defendants as kind and loving people and good citizens at heart, despite their troubles in court.

Sandy Murphy apologized during her unsworn statement.

Then it was time for Sandy Murphy to speak in what is known as an "unsworn statement." She was not allowed to profess her innocence. Tearfully reading from a handwritten statement, she apologized to everyone.

"I know you haven't had a chance to hear from me yet. But I've been very anxious to share the truth—the truth about what happened to Teddy. Regretfully, I did not testify, and now I can see that was a mistake. But instead of looking at what could have been, I can only look at what will be.

"… As I look about the room today I see pain and suffering all around me: Bonnie for the loss of her father; Becky, Brenda, and Jack for the loss of their brother; the Fechsers and all the family and friends that were touched by Teddy's life. For the Tabish family, who have also suffered the loss of a son, a husband, a brother, and an uncle, and for Amanda and Kyle for the loss of their father. For my family, for my parents and my brothers and sisters. …

"For my loss, for the loss of my Teddy 'Ruxpin.' He was the man that swept me off my feet. I thought he was my fix-it man. I thought he would fill the hole in my heart. I thought he would always love and protect me.

"… Last night I lay in my bed thinking of what I wanted to say here today, and there was one thing that stuck out in my mind. There was something that I need to do for me. I want to say that I'm sorry to the Binion family, but most of all I'm sorry to Bonnie, and I'm sorry for the day I walked out that door on September 17th and left him there alone. And I'm sorry today for not being there when he needed me the most."

Rick Tabish appeared less remorseful during his statement.

Rick Tabish, in his endless attempt to persuade and cajole, couldn't resist complimenting the jury and the attorneys on their efforts.

" … I had the attitude nothing was good enough, and when the verdict came back, it was good enough. Everybody's worked for me. I've taken advantage of everybody's hard work. And I'm sorry, but in return what I have to say is I'm proud of who I am. You guys have returned a verdict on me. That's your decision. I'm going to have to live with that decision. I'm man enough to live with that decision."

"... I'm not perfect by all means. I'm not standing here saying I'm perfect. I've made my mistakes. ... I have no real regrets about anything I did except getting involved in this situation. My heart's broke because everybody else is destroyed. If I could go spend the rest of my life in prison, or if I could give my life so that my mother, my two brothers that sat up there crying, could live their lives without knowing that their brother is going to prison for the rest of his, I would do it. I'm not that selfish of a man.

"My heart's out to the Binion family, I mean that sincerely," he said, not sounding terribly sincere.

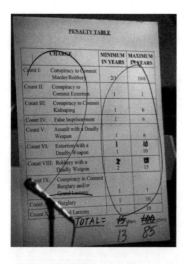

Five days later, the jury determined that Rick Tabish and Sandy Murphy should receive sentences of life with the possibility of parole after 20 years. In the weeks that followed, during additional sentencing hearings, they received additional time in connection with the attempted theft of the $7 million silver fortune.

For the first time since the trial began, Chief Deputy District Attorney David Roger broke his silence.

"I feel that justice has been served," said the prosecutor, whose name was already being mentioned for possible judgeships and even a future as the Clark County District Attorney.

Other principals weighed in with their own versions of the verdicts and sentences. Investigator Tom Dillard commented, "I believed a murder had been committed from the day I walked into the house. The crime scene, in my opinion, was clearly staged. When I saw the crime-scene photos, I was pretty convinced there had been a homicide. Whether it could be proven or not was another matter."

Rick Tabish's younger brother Greg, who'd attended each day of the trial and pleaded for his brother's life during the sentencing phase, said, "As God is my witness, my brother is an innocent man."

Tabish's mother Lani added, "It's a sad day when you have to beg for your child's life."

Attorney Harry Claiborne, who had represented the Binion family for nearly 40 years and had delivered the eulogy at Ted Binion's funeral, said, "I applaud their verdict. There is no question in my mind that these two young people killed Ted Binion and they were motivated by greed. The most horrible part is their attitude. They were arrogant and cavalier about the whole thing. This verdict won't bring Ted Binion back. It is really sad."

"There is pain and suffering from all four corners of this courtroom," said prosecutor David Wall, summing up the prevailing sentiment. "But recall that responsibility for that suffering is at the feet of Sandy Murphy and Rick Tabish."

◊ ◊ ◊

"Finito!"

There were still a few details for Judge Bonaventure to dispose of, but by September 15 defendants David Mattsen, Steven Wadkins, John Joseph, and Michael Milot had all accepted plea agreements to that allowed them to accept gross misdemeanor convictions and avoid jail time. Judge Bonaventure appeared anxious to finally close what had been deemed Southern Nevada's trial of the century.

"That's it," the judge said at last. "Finito."

Not long afterward, attorneys for Sandy Murphy and Rick Tabish filed an appeal of their murder convictions citing possible juror misconduct, a failure of the judge to sever the defendants' cases into separate trials, and a lack of sufficient evidence to establish guilt beyond a reasonable doubt. The appeals are making their way slowly through the Nevada Supreme Court.

From prison, the defendants continued to maintain their innocence.

Wherever he was, Ted Binion could rest easy knowing that many people would remember the story of his life, and that in death he had finally become something that had eluded him in life: a Las Vegas legend.

The Ted Binion
Murder Trial

1999—2000

Binion Case Timeline

1995

February—Sandy Murphy loses money gambling at Caesars Palace, begins working in Las Vegas to repay her debts.

March 7—Sandy Murphy moves into Ted Binion's house at 2408 Palomino Lane.

1997

May—Binion's gaming license is suspended due to his drug abuse. He is ordered to undergo daily drug testing.

1998

March—Nevada Gaming Commission revokes Binion's gaming license, citing his drug abuse and ties to organized-crime figures.

June 4—Rick Tabish finishes Pahrump vault Binion hired him to build for storing $7 million worth of silver bars and coins. Tabish and Binion are the only two people with the combination to the vault.

September 17—Ted Binion dies.

September 19—Rick Tabish, David Mattsen, and Michael Milot are caught in Pahrump digging up the silver.

September 23—Tom Dillard begins investigating Binion's death on behalf of his estate.

September 29—Tabish, Milot, and Mattsen are charged with crimes related to the theft of Binion's silver.

December 22—Chief Deputy District Attorney David Roger is assigned to the Binion case.

1999

February 11—Murphy refuses to answer questions during a Binion-estate probate hearing. She invokes her Fifth Amendment right more than 200 times during the hearing.

March 15—Binion's death declared a homicide by the Clark County Coroner.

June 14—Tabish and Murphy charged with death of Binion.

June 24—Tabish and Murphy arrested on murder charges.

August 14—Additional charges filed against Tabish and Murphy related to the alleged extortion of Leo Casey. John Joseph and Steve Wadkins are named in charges, which are later dropped against Murphy.

November 2—Murphy's attorney John Momot files a motion alleging Clark County Detention Center officials illegally obtained her panties.

November 15—Judge Joseph Bonaventure rules Murphy failed to establish that jail officials absconded with her undergarment.

2000

March 24—Muphy ordered jailed for duration of trial for violating house arrest.

March 27—Jury selection begins.

March 31—Opening statements.

April 3—Doris Kilmer Binion testifies about her tumultuous relationship with Binion.

April 4—Kurt Gratzer testifies that Tabish wanted to hire him to kill Binion.

April 7—Leo Casey testifies to Tabish extortion.

April 13—Bonnie Binion testifies.

April 18—Dr. Michael Baden testifies that Binion was suffocated.

April 26—Prosecution rests.

April 26—Jason Frazer testifies that Tabish tried to purchase alibi witnesses.

April 28—Jurors review silver fortune.

May 3—Dr. Cyril Wecht testifies that Binion likely committed suicide.

May 5—Defense rests.

May 10—At 1 p.m., the jury begins deliberations.

May 19—At 4:30 p.m., jury returns verdict: Tabish and Murphy guilty on all counts.

May 24—Tabish and Murphy receive life with the possibility of parole.

September 15—Bonaventure closes main murder case.

September 22—Treasure hunt in Pahrump turns up no silver.

October 5—Bonaventure finishes the last details of the case.

The Preliminary Hearing

August 1999—September 1999

At a preliminary hearing, evidence need not rise to the standard of "beyond a reasonable doubt" that is a prerequisite to convict at trial. Instead, a judge reviews a portion of the physical evidence and witness testimony before determining whether there is "probable cause" to believe a crime has been committed, and whether the defendants were responsible for committing the crime.

As he arrived in chains wearing his Clark County Detention Center uniform just days after his arrest, Rick Tabish flashed what would become his trademark look of contempt. Tabish began weightlifting soon after being jailed for the murder of Ted Binion. Justice of the Peace Jennifer Togliatti conducted the month-long preliminary hearing, one of the longest in the history of the Southern Nevada justice system, before ruling that there was enough evidence against the defendants to proceed to trial.

Ken and Sandra Murphy, bottom, took cues from their daughter, who blew them kisses and mouthed, "I love you." The similarities in the names of daughter and stepmother caused confusion.

Even the abbreviated nature of the preliminary process got emotional for Murphy, who was seen weeping for the first of dozens of times, and Tabish, who had to be admonished to remain silent at the defense table by his lawyer at the time, Steve Wolfson.

At the same time, the Binion estate was contesting Ted Binion's will, which named Murphy as the inheritor of the $900,000 home on Palomino Lane and all its contents. Former U.S. District Judge and Binion estate lawyer Harry Claiborne, right, was happy to bait Tabish during probate hearings.

While Murphy's house arrest status enabled her to dress for court in flashy designer clothes, Tabish was denied bail and forced to wear jailhouse garb prior to trial.

With the financial assistance of an 80-year-old Irish businessman named William Fuller, who followed her into court on several occasions, Murphy initially remained free. Although Fuller declined to be interviewed at length by the press, he said through intermediaries that he believed Murphy was an innocent young woman; all he was interested in was justice.

Potential ramifications escape Murphy

Listen closely, and you can almost hear the sound of shovels tunneling or a hacksaw nipping at metal bars. If I didn't know better, I'd swear Rick Tabish and Sandra Murphy were trying to break into the penitentiary.

Call it a cheap psychological profile from a two-bit newsy, but I still get the feeling Murphy is not clearly aware that her life is on the line and that appearances count for something beyond attracting boyfriends and benefactors. ...

—John L. Smith
Las Vegas Review-Journal

Judge Togliatti refused to sever the charges against Murphy, who had no previous criminal record, and Tabish, a twice-convicted felon.

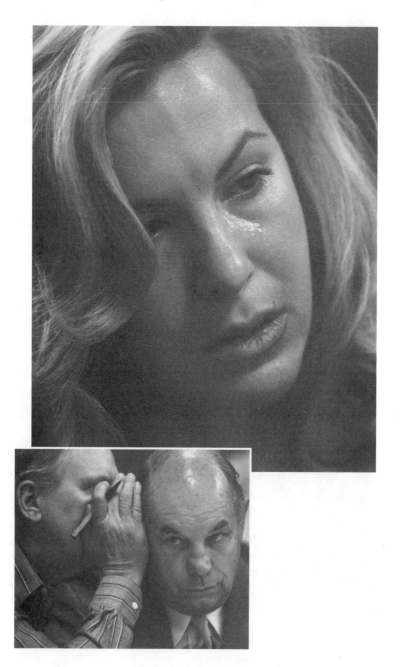

The emotional preliminary hearing, which was covered extensively on television and in the press, stoked the public's interest in the case at a time many in Southern Nevada were undecided whether Ted Binion had been murdered or was the victim of his own excesses. Former Binion ranch foreman David Mattsen, seen whispering to attorney James "Bucky" Buchanan, opposite, was charged in the $7 million silver theft and claimed to know what really happened to Binion. Clark County Chief Medical Examiner Dr. Lary Simms, above, testified that Binion was the victim of a homicide-related drug overdose. His determination would be challenged later by estate forensic pathologist Dr. Michael Baden.

With Rick Tabish showing signs that jail was wearing on him, between crying jags Sandy Murphy flirted with photographers, visited with her co-defendant's parents, and dined on gourmet lunches courtesy of the posh Aristocrat restaurant. Murphy caused a stir when she painted her court-ordered ankle monitor to match her shoes and outfit. Many in the public viewed her attitude, under the grim circumstances, as one of extreme arrogance and disregard for the man she had sworn she loved.

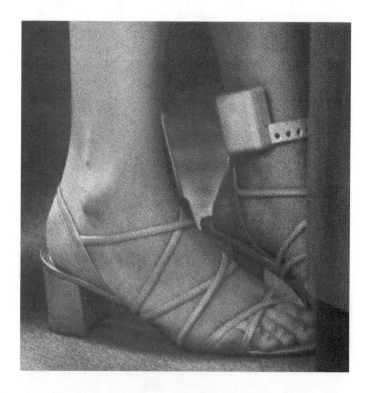

Murphy said that she spray-painted her ankle monitor from black to beige to match her outfit that day. Until Judge Togliatti stepped in to admonish her, she said she hadn't decided whether to continue changing its color daily.

Murphy turns away as attorney Steve Wolfson shows
Tabish photos from the Binion autopsy.

Frank Tabish (Rick's father) greets Sandy Murphy, who is carrying a catered lunch from the
Aristocrat, as Rick's brother, Greg, looks on. Murphy remained outwardly lighthearted throughout much of the preliminary hearing.

Take Sandy out of the will if she doesn't kill me tonight. If I'm dead, you'll know what happened.

—Ted Binion
to Jim Brown

Binion's friend and attorney Richard Wright, opposite top, found himself in the unfamiliar position of being asked to answer questions under oath during the preliminary hearing. He held a strong belief that Binion had been murdered and that Tabish and Murphy were responsible. Binion estate attorney Jim Brown, opposite bottom, appeared far more nervous as he discussed details of the will and the conversation he claimed had taken place between himself and Binion only a day before the casino man's death. In that conversation, Brown said Binion told him to take Murphy out of the will if she didn't kill him. Meanwhile, Nye County Sheriff Wade Lieseke, above, denied that he'd agreed to allow Tabish access to Binion's Pahrump ranch only a day after his death.

Binion-case bit players Steven Wadkins, left, and John Joseph, appeared to have no link to the homicide, but instead found themselves caught up in the kidnapping, beating and extortion of an oddball mining consultant named Leo Casey.

Michael Milot was connected to Tabish after agreeing to help him remove Binion's silver fortune from the Pahrump vault. He was not charged in either the murder or the Casey extortion.

Ever the cowhand, David Mattsen dressed in blue jeans and casual hats for the preliminary hearing, but was clearly more emotional than the other silver-theft defendants.

In a moment of courtroom musical chairs, Tabish changed lawyers from Wolfson to Louis Palazzo (above right), who had originally represented him. Murphy, meanwhile, used attorneys David Chesnoff, Oscar Goodman, and Gardner Jolly for the estate case, and Bill Terry, shown here, during the preliminary hearing.

In one of the preliminary hearing's high-profile asides, Murphy was taken ill from food poisoning after eating chicken enchiladas she'd prepared for her sister the night before. After showing up for court 15 minutes late and being allowed to leave once during the proceedings, she was asked if it was court that was making her sick. She responded, "Oh no, court doesn't bother me."

District Attorney Stewart Bell, left, and downtown casino owner Jackie Gaughan observed the preliminary hearing from the rear of the courtroom.

Casino man remembers talented, troubled Binion

Jackie Gaughan sat quietly in the back of the courtroom, listening to the attorneys banter and bluster and jockey for position. The octogenarian casino legend had come to court in his dice tie and natty sport coat to hear strangers talk about the life of his friend Ted Binion. Jackie remembered Ted at about age 5, dropping by the casino and soaking up the atmosphere.

"He was always a good fella," Gaughan recalled. "He was very bright, very talented, especially when it came to those cheaters and stuff."

And very troubled. Gaughan is careful to protect the memory of his friend, but there are no secrets where Binion's drug use was concerned. Gaughan recalled a young Ted Binion's attempt to join the Air Force.

"He couldn't make it," Gaughan said in the hall outside court. "He couldn't pass the drug test." ...

—John L. Smith
Las Vegas Review-Journal

Pre-Trial Hearings

September 1999—March 2000

Prior to trial, court time is set aside to entertain motions in a criminal case. Among the many requests attorneys for Tabish and Murphy made of Judge Bonaventure was for a change of venue due to undue pretrial coverage of the case in the media. Although the judge placed a temporary gag order on participants, he lifted it once it was determined the defendants were proceeding to trial.

After the preliminary hearing, the case moved to District Judge Joseph Bonaventure's court. Bonaventure admonished Murphy, who at trial would be represented by attorney John Momot, opposite top, not to take the strict terms of her house arrest status lightly. She was jailed for 10 days after violating a condition of her bail by breaking her curfew.

As the seriousness of their situation finally began sinking in, the demeanor of the defendants changed noticeably.

A series of showdowns took place in Bonaventure's court, with the defense coming up short on nearly every occasion. Murphy took an active role in the defense effort, whispering incessantly throughout the proceedings.

Defense attempts to have Binion estate private investigator Tom Dillard, right, declared "an agent of the state," in essence a police officer, were shot down by Bonaventure despite the fact the former Metro Homicide investigator had interviewed more than 100 witnesses and turned over his findings to the police. While his essential role in the case was widely acknowledged by the prosecution, and reluctantly admitted by the defense, Dillard was never called to testify at trial. More importantly, not one of his tape-recorded interviews were credibly disputed.

Judge Joe

Around District Court, Judge Joseph Bonaventure was known as a tough, no-nonsense guy who had remained true to his working-class roots. He has been described by trial lawyer Dominic Gentile as a judge who rules "with an iron fist wrapped in a velvet glove."

The Ted Binion murder case not only enhanced that image, but also revealed Bonaventure as a seasoned jurist who was unruffled by either the media spotlight or the complex nature of the largely circumstantial case.

"I don't think there's been anything like this case ever, in terms of being highly publicized," Bonaventure said in an interview in early 2001.

"It seems to me that the trial gave the Las Vegas community an opportunity to get an inside view of their justice system at work. That was a positive aspect of the trial."

Judging by the feedback Bonaventure received, a majority of the public was pleased with his to-the-point approach. The judge's office was inundated with hundreds of letters and e-mail from citizens who followed his every move.

"It was a pretty complex case, and certainly had a lot of sensationalism involved," Bonaventure said. "Thank God I had the experience that I did. I think if a civil judge or a judge with one or two years on the bench had this case, it would have been very difficult for them because this one was complex and immense and touched on every criminal issue I've had in 22 years. It was grueling, and I'm thankful for my staff and my clerk, Al Lasso, who is my right arm.

"I feel like I ran the Binion case like I have every other case. People say I'm rough, but I try to be fair."

Estate private investigator Tom Dillard, above, a retired Metro Homicide Bureau detective, had vast experience in court. His work was invaluable to the investigation and prosecution of Murphy and Tabish. Combined with the testimony of Jason Frazer, right, who admitted under a grant of immunity that he had helped arrange to pay for alibi witnesses for Tabish, it was enough to give the defendants headaches.

Attorney John Momot had seen better days. After repeatedly violating conditions of her court-ordered house arrest, Murphy was remanded to custody despite Momot's best argument. Tabish attorney Louis Palazzo spent much of his time being frustrated by Judge Bonaventure.

Her house-arrest privileges rescinded for good, Sandy Murphy is led back to jail. The beginning of Murphy's incarceration marked the end of her glamorous presence in court, as she no longer had access to her hairstylist and wardrobe.

William Fuller was Sandy Murphy's mysterious benefactor. Bottom, Fuller is flanked by Murphy's parents.

Murphy's silent backer
hopes justice speaks clearly

The Irish have a legendary oral tradition, but for the most part, Dubliner William Fuller has remained silent about his substantial financial support of Sandy Murphy.

For Murphy, the immensely generous Fuller appeared at a most opportune time, basically paying for her costly defense, which has been estimated in the neighborhood of $1 million.

Fuller, who has been a part-time Las Vegas resident for 30 years, recalled meeting Murphy after she became the subject of intense law enforcement and media scrutiny. He said it was by chance that he saw her in a television newsclip being escorted by the cops, and he eventually learned that she frequented the Aristocrat restaurant near Binion's Palomino Lane home. A meeting was arranged through an Aristocrat employee.

In short order, Fuller became Murphy's legal benefactor. He went to the extent of leasing her an apartment, but has insisted that he was only trying to give a break to a young woman he believed to be innocent.

... Of the mystery that surrounds him, Fuller just shrugs. He's been a legitimate businessman and has no dealings with underworld characters, speculation of which has circulated in some segments of the press.

"I have nothing to do with mobsters or anything like that," Fuller said. "I'm just an ornery old man."

—John L. Smith
Las Vegas Review-Journal

Sandy's Secret

While Sandy Murphy claimed to be offended by all the media attention she was receiving, there were moments she clearly reveled in her celebrity as the leggy accused killer.

Privately, she confided to friends about the lucrative potential of turning her story into a movie, and she had entered into negotiations to sell the rights to her version of the Binion affair. Interested parties ranged from "Bay Watch" producer Michael Berk and his wife, Michele, to "Casino" author Nick Pileggi and casino Black Book member Joey Cusumano.

But it was the tale of Murphy's missing black panties that defined her as a salacious sex symbol.

Murphy claimed her panties turned up missing after she was returned to the Clark County Detention Center for violating the conditions of her house arrest. She enlisted her attorney, John Momot, to compel jail officials to conduct a search for the missing underwear.

Somehow, Momot managed to keep a straight face when he submitted a brief to District Judge Joseph Bonaventure requesting an evidentiary hearing. But he couldn't help taking advantage of the opportunity when he requested that Bonaventure spend court time to "get to the bottom of this matter."

Police and prosecutors claimed that the panty story was little more than an attempt by the defendant to turn the proceeding into a farce—or a jailhouse version of a Victoria's Secret advertisement—and in the end Bonaventure agreed.

The black panties were never recovered, but rumors were rampant that Murphy would develop her own line of lingerie.

Sandy's Secret, perhaps?

The Trial

March 2000—May 2000

> *In a criminal trial, 12 jurors must determine whether the evidence presented proves guilt "beyond a reasonable doubt." Anything less, and they must vote to acquit. In order to convict, the vote must be unanimous.*

The main trial convened on March 31 amid a circus atmosphere. In an inspired move, prosecutors projected Ted Binion's image on a large screen as a reminder that, despite all the distractions, a man was dead. The photo below provided one of the trial's most compelling images, as Sandy Murphy walked in front of the projection and her shadow fell over Binion's face.

Facing Page: Courthouse personnel set up a ticket system (top) for the first day of trial, and citizens lined up early for a seat. Inside the courtroom (center), the prosecution, left, and defense, right, prepared for opening statements. The case would mark the first time Court TV used all remote-control cameras (bottom), which enabled photographer Dennis Lynch to remain seated in the back of the courtroom.

THE PROSECUTION

Chief Deputy District Attorney David Wall

THE PROSECUTION

Chief Deputy District Attorney David Roger

THE DEFENSE

John Momot
Lead Defense Attorney for Sandy Murphy

THE DEFENSE

Louis Palazzo
Lead Defense Attorney for Rick Tabish

District Attorneys Wall and Roger took a chance when they called Ted Binion's ex-wife, Doris Kilmer Binion, to the witness stand early in the proceedings. The couple's 29-year relationship had been punctuated by Ted Binion's struggle with drug addiction, propensity for violence, and occasional threat of suicide. While her testimony appeared to bolster the confidence of the defense, which claimed Binion had committed suicide, it did not change the prosecution's contention that a murder had been committed.

Ex-wife gives jury harsh look at Ted Binion's character

The tears rolled down Doris Kilmer Binion's face Monday as she recounted a few of the incidents of abuse she had taken at the hands of her husband, Ted Binion, during their tumultuous 29-year relationship.

All of the good times and financial rewards she had enjoyed with Binion faded as she described being tormented, battered, knocked to the ground, and kicked until she suffered a cracked rib in March 1995, shortly before she left their Palomino Lane home and filed for divorce.

Although it was the prosecution's intention to offer her as a witness who could characterize murder defendant Sandy Murphy as a home wrecker, it became brutally obvious that the dwelling at 2804 Palomino Lane was already a house of horrors. ...

—John L. Smith
Las Vegas Review-Journal

Montana resident Kurt Gratzer, top, had been a friend of Rick Tabish's since childhood. But Gratzer testified that Tabish had solicited him to murder a Las Vegas casino owner, presumed to be Ted Binion. Although the credibility of Gratzer's testimony was highly suspect, investigators found several persons who helped corroborate his statements. Missoula pharmacist Jon Berman, bottom left, testified that Gratzer had asked him questions about a lethal dose of a prescription drug, and Tim Boileau, bottom right, swore Gratzer had briefly discussed the Tabish murder plot prior to Binion's death.

Murphy was displeased with her defense team's cross-examination of Gratzer. Sitting in the jury box after the day's adjournment, she complains to Momot that the defense went too easy.

Manicurist Deanna Perry testified that she had waited on Sandy Murphy and her girlfriend, Linda Carroll, shortly before Binion's death. In that conversation, Perry reported overhearing Murphy complaining about Binion and predicting his death of a heroin overdose. Perry also told the court Murphy talked about bringing a new boyfriend to a Las Vegas charity gala.

Beverly Hills Hotel reservations clerk Natalie Vogt, explained resort records that showed Tabish and Murphy appeared to be sharing a romantic weekend there shortly before Binion's death. Vogt had been a contestant on the controversial television special "Who

Wants to Marry a Millionaire?" It led some skeptics to observe that Vogt and Murphy had something in common.

Norm Knows

The trial provided fodder for many of Las Vegas' print journalists. Popular *Review-Journal* columnist Norm Clarke took delight in relating juicy gossip, and didn't miss his chance with Vogt:

"Upon sitting in the witness chair, Vogt addressed the courtroom with a chirpy, 'Hello everybody!' She left the stand with a 'Good-bye everybody!'

"During testimony, Vogt was asked abut the ritzy Peninsula Hotel, where Murphy and co-defendant Rick Tabish stayed in an $825-a-night suite: 'It's a five-star, five-diamond hotel, the only five-star, five-diamond hotel, and it has 196 rooms, and it's an excellent hotel.'

"Bonaventure wasn't pleased. 'This is not a free commercial here now, you know,' the judge said."

Early damaging testimony did little to dampen the defendants' outward confidence. "How do you expect someone to act when they're not guilty?" Ken Murphy, Sandy's father, asked.

Hubris

The courtroom conduct of Murphy and Tabish was often termed cocky, but it couldn't match the defendants' brazen actions prior to their arrests. Rather than try to conceal a relationship that, at the time, they were denying, the couple actually flaunted it—they were often seen shopping or dining together. They reached the pinnacle of their hubris when they took time to entertain a *Gentlemen's Quarterly* writer. The bizarre nine-page article, published in December 1999, detailed the trio's cavorting, including a night at a local topless cabaret, during which the publicity-hungry couple purchased lap dances for the writer.

Without a smoking gun, the Binion murder trial relied heavily on circumstantial evidence. After Leo Casey demostrated how Tabish allegedly battered him with a phone book, Dr. Enrique Lacayo, bottom, admitted under oath that he had prescribed the Xanax that contributed to Binion's death.

Former Las Vegas Mayor Jan Laverty Jones, top, testified that she received a $40,000 campaign contribution from Binion shortly before his death, and real estate agent Barbara Brown, bottom, told the court Sandy Murphy was frantic during a brief phone call they had around noon on September 17. Brown recalled Murphy saying, "Nobody understands what it has been like living with a drug addict."

Sandy Murphy found herself facing a barrage of damaging testimony. Throughout the trial, Murphy became emotional whenever Ted Binion's heroin use or the Palomino house were discussed.

Peter Sheridan, a rock guitarist turned heroin junkie and dealer, told the court he sold Binion black tar the night before he died. Binion had been in the company of Tabish and Murphy.

Gardener Tom Loveday described the strange quiet, drawn drapes, and family dogs scratching nervously at the sliding-glass window that led to the den where Binion was found.

Maid Mary Montoya-Gascoigne tells the court about Murphy's instructions not to come to work at the Palomino Lane house on September 17, 1998.

Las Vegas Metropolitan Police crime-scene analyst Mike Perkins' testimony was of particular interest to investigators. Opposite, he notes the "mortuary pose" of the body, and pinpoints its location in the house. Perkins also testified, top, that he had recoverd traces of the balloons that contained the heroin Binion smoked, as well as a macabre figure with "RIP" written on it that was positioned in front of Binion's home.

Ted Binion's 19-year-old daughter, Bonnie, described her father as a good man with a thirst for knowledge and a weakness for Sandy Murphy.

Bonnie's Bombshell

The testimony of Ted Binion's daughter, Bonnie, produced some of the most poignant moments of the lengthy trial.

Her testimony was important, as she not only established the cash wealth that had been present at Binion's home—"he often kept money in the cooler ... in the boat ... in the drawers in his bathroom ... in the pockets of his suits in the closet, and there was an urn in the den and a box in his bedroom that he often kept money in"—but noted for the court that she had never seen her father lie on the floor for any reason. On September 17, 1998, Binion's home contained little money, and his body was found on a sleeping mat in the den.

The young Ms. Binion maintained her composure throughout most of her time on the witness stand, but eventually sobbed as David Roger delved into her relationship with her father.

"Growing up, he spent most of his time with me, seven days a week, doing things all the time," she told the court. "He was incredibly intelligent. He tried to explain his ways of doing math and multiplication in his head. It was amazing what he could do with numbers. He had a massive knowledge of history and politics."

She also addressed her tumultuous relationship with Sandy Murphy:

"She no longer wanted me to return to the house. She had threatened to kill both of us. [During an incident outside the Palomino Lane home in June 1998] my father came out of the house and he got in the car and Miss Murphy came outside, and she was screaming and yelling at him and me. She didn't want me on her property and [said] that she would call the police if I didn't leave. ... She called me a bitch."

Murphy continued to be an active presence in the courtroom researching documents and contributing input during the proceedings. As the trial wore on, her nervous note writing and chatter began to irritate Judge Bonaventure.

A key point in the trial was the airing of a videotape, shot by an attorney friend of Murphy's, which showed her taking an inventory of items in the Palomino house she shared with Binion. The video, shot just one day after the death, depicted Murphy not as a grieving spouse but as a foul-mouthed gold-digger who was more interested in preventing the Binions from taking what she believed was rightfully hers under the conditions of Binion's will. The damning footage caused Murphy to lay her head on the courtroom table, sobbing.

Chief Clark County Medical Examiner Dr. Lary Simms, who performed the autopsy of Ted Binion, ruled the death a homicide due to a forced overdose of heroin and the prescription sedative Xanax. Because his testimony differed with prosecution expert Dr. Michael Baden, who determined Binion had been suffocated and had not ingested enough drugs to cause his death, Simms became a prime target of the defense. During Simms' testimony, Murphy often pouted to show her disdain.

In another of the trial's noteworthy asides, court was interrupted after lunch on April 17, when it was discovered that Golden Nugget bellhop Richard Sueno, pictured above with unamused Bailiff Matt Diamond, shouted during a break that the defendants were innocent. A hearing determined that none of the jurors were influenced by Sueno.

While there were always people lined up for tickets to the trial, the crowds were particularly heavy during the testimony of renowned forensic pathologist Dr. Michael Baden, who had an almost cult-like following due to his television show on HBO.

Sandy Murphy reads Dr. Baden's book, *Unnatural Death—Confessions of a Medical Examiner*, during his testimony.

Michael Baden became a focal point of the prosecution's case and provided a formidable challenge to the defense. A veteran of hundreds of courtroom appearances and thousands of autopsies, Baden testified that he believed Binion had died from a method of suffocation known as "Burkeing," in which the lungs and mouth are constricted to the point that the victim suffocates. Wily courtroom veteran James Shellow, left, was unable to budge Baden from his opinions, despite the medical expert's admission that he hadn't examined Binion's corpse.

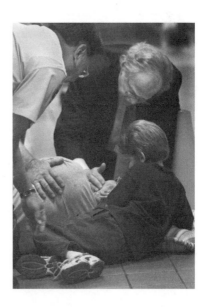

During a break in his testimony, Baden came to the aid of Ann Davis, who suffered a seizure after coming to court with her young son, Christopher.

In a case full of hired guns, defense consultant William L. Cassidy was perhaps the most intriguing. Cassidy, pictured (right) in the top photo with attorney Steve Stein, irritated the prosecution with his accusations of unethical conduct. At the same time, Cassidy's Trial Consultants of Nevada was busy buying ethically questionable advertising during breaks in the televised trial coverage, and taking daily public-opinion surveys of the efforts of the prosecution and

defense. At one point, Cassidy was accused of threatening the life of private detective Tom Dillard. The allegation resulted in multiple hearings and provided a sideshow to the legal theater that seemed to grow stranger by the day.

William Cassidy hugs Sandy Murphy.

Shadowy consultant adds to trial's intrigue

It's almost as if defense consultant William L. Cassidy slipped off the set of Casablanca and stepped onto the scene at the Ted Binion murder trial.

With his slight frame, thick mustache and thicker eyeglasses, the defense team's ghostly gaunt gunslinger casts a shadow of intrigue whether sitting next to defendant Sandy Murphy or chain smoking outside the courtroom. His heavy gold jewelry, $3,000 suits, and full-time driver add to the air.

It's easy to forget that he did not come to our desert for the waters, but to work with former defense attorney turned Las Vegas Mayor, Oscar Goodman. When Goodman was elected by a landslide, Cassidy accompanied him to City Hall as a senior staff member.

When Murphy's defense appeared to be stalling several weeks ago, Cassidy returned to work her case.

… "Before I opened up and blasted, I didn't have a care in the world in this case," Cassidy says. "Then I began questioning the quality of the evidence in this case and the district attorney, and now I'm being subpoenaed in this case. Who's got an ethical question for me, Stew Bell? I've got an ethical question for you."

—John L. Smith
Las Vegas Review-Journal

Each prosecution witness carried in his testimony a piece of the Binion puzzle. Nye County Sheriff's Office Sgt. Ed Howard, top, caught Tabish lying about the real reason his crew had taken heavy equipment to Binion's Pahrump property; the excavated silver was discovered inside the truck (pictured). His testimony was corroborated by Deputy Steve Huggins, lower left. William Alder, lower right, explained that he helped Binion move the silver fortune from the Horseshoe to the Pahrump vault.

" The trouble Rick was in, I didn't really want the coins. "

—Dennis Rehbein

Dennis Rehbein agreed to loan $25,000 to his brother-in-law, Rick Tabish, and received bags of silver coins as collateral. The silver had come from Binion's house on Palomino Lane.

Meanwhile, the testimony of attorney Tom Standish, left, appeared to corroborate, in part, Tabish's claim that Binion had wanted him to move the silver fortune after his death. Tonya Cropp, right, worked briefly as Binion's secretary and, after admitting she had lied during a previous grand jury appearance, told the court that she had spoken with Binion shortly before his death about his relationship with Murphy.

"My life is on the line. We have to fight fire with fire," Rick Tabish wrote in a note to Jason Frazer, a friend and business associate. Frazer was arrested as a material witness in the case. After being granted immunity, he admitted participating in a plot to provide alibi witnesses for Tabish. He also said Tabish instructed him to pay those who agreed to provide an alibi, as well as damaging testimony against estate investigator Tom Dillard.

" It was Ted Binion's silver that he was going to get to solve all his probems. "

—David Roger, referencing
Rick Tabish's $1.6 million debt

At the heart of the motive for the crime alleged by the prosecution was the silver. Ted Binion's silver fortune weighed approximately 48,000 pounds and was worth an estimated $7 million. The silver consisted of coins, some of them rare, and dozens of bars of various sizes.

When the defense began calling its witnesses, Sandra Murphy attempted to paint a sympathetic portrait of her stepdaughter, one very different from the person depicted on a videotape taken after Binion's death.

> *I would venture to say that Michael [Baden] is always correct in his findings, except, of course, when I'm testifying for the other side.*
>
> —Dr. Cyril Wecht

Defense forensic pathologist Cyril Wecht was brought in to counter the damaging testimony of Simms and Baden, who differed on the cause of death but agreed that Binion had been a victim of homicide. Wecht declared that the ruptured blood vessels, known as petechiae, that could have been signs of suffocation were not present in Binion's eyes. Wecht admitted that he was a friend and admirer of Baden and, like him, had testified as a paid professional witness for years.

Defense crime-scene expert Paul Dougherty, top, testified that Metro did an unprofessional job in securing the crime scene on September 17, 1998. Dentist and State Senator Ray Rawson, bottom left, Dr. Robert Bucklin, bottom right, and Dr. Jack Snyder, opposite, gave their opinions that Binion was not a victim of homicide.

In general, the defense's battery of experts proved ineffective. Snyder, in particular, came off as cocky and combative in his attacks on Dr. Michael Baden.

Sniping Snyder

Dr. Jack Snyder testified for the defense that Binion died of a drug overdose arising from the combined effects of heroin, Xanax and Valium.

"It's a recipe for disaster," the pathologist and toxicologist said. "You get a triple whammy." Soft-spoken and deferential when questioned by defense attorneys, Snyder underwent a transformation when confronted by the prosecution. His tone became shrill, and he spoke so quickly his words seemed to meld together. Those seated in the increasingly vocal public section of the gallery openly rooted against Snyder, and some jurors were heard groaning when he attacked the expertise of prosecution expert Dr. Michael Baden.

Baden, who has performed about 20,000 autopsies, testified that he has conducted more autopsies in heroin-related deaths than anyone in the country. Snyder, who has performed a total of 500 autopsies, said Baden's experience is rooted in the 1960s and 1970s. "He's 40 years behind the times?" Chief Deputy District Attorney David Wall asked. "Yes, that's exactly right," Snyder replied.

The defense's problems mounted, even with their own witnesses on the stand. Las Vegas Fire Department emergency medical technician Ken Dickinson, top, and ambulance company paramedic Richard Resnick, bottom, testified that a mark found on Binion's chest was not the result of a sternum rub, which is performed in an effort to revive a patient. During the course of this testimony, a videotape of Murphy's disingenuous "boo-hooing" at the hospital was shown, eliciting yet another sobbing episode from Murphy, opposite.

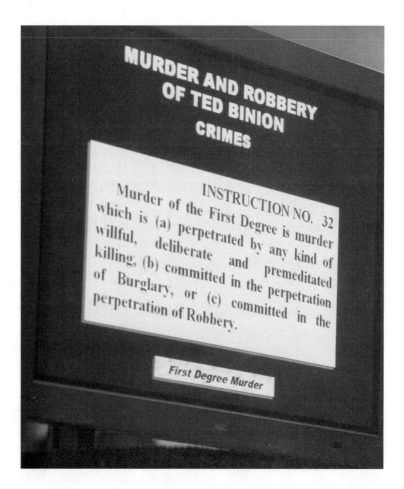

With testimony from both sides concluded, the trial moved to the summations.

"*The true fact is, [Murphy] did not kill Ted Binion. But the sad fact is, Ted Binion did die of a conspiracy. It was a conspiracy between himself and heroin. I don't want to let Ted Binion's addiction destroy Sandy Murphy.*"

—**John Momot**

"*Ted Binion did not have a bad day shaving. He had a bad day because someone was killing him by suffocating him. … They stole every-thing Ted Binion had, including his life.*"

—**David Roger**

"*[It's about] money, love, greed, lust—classic motives for murder.*"

—**David Wall**

"*There is no murder here.*"

—**Louis Palazzo**

TED BINION WAS
DRUGGED AND
SUFFOCATED BY
HIS KILLERS

At its essence, the prosecution's closing argument was simple: homicide by drugs and suffocation. John Momot confers with Tabish and Murphy; the prosecution's assertion is displayed on the screen in foreground.

At top, John Momot attempts to explain the defintion of the law to the jury during closing arguments. Center, attorney Tom Pitaro, who represented Steven Wadkins in the extortion of Leo Casey, sat with the defense during closing arguments. Bottom, Judge Bonaventure made life difficult for attorney Louis Palazzo—here he denies Palazzo's request to hit Rick Tabish with the Yellow Pages.

Chief Deputy District Attorney David Wall put on an impressive display when explaining Judge Bonaventure's jury instructions; District Attorney Stewart Bell took in the proceedings, below.

Top, former Horseshoe owner Jack Binion, flanked by Bonnie Binion (left) and Doris Kilmer Binion, did not set foot in the courtroom until the final hours. Bonnie was lauded by courtroom observers for her emotional but effective testimony. Meanwhile, Becky Behnen, below, kept a close watch on the closing arguments from her office at the Horseshoe.

The closing arguments were an opportunity for methodical Chief Deputy District Attorney David Roger to shine.

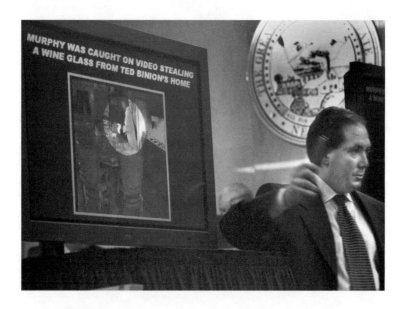

Binion prosecutor's style focuses jury on his substance

Even with the aid of computer-generated graphics, Chief Deputy District Attorney David Roger didn't leave the jury wide-eyed and breathless during his closing argument Monday in the Ted Binion murder trial.

As ever, Roger worked slowly, like a stone mason chipping through granite. Roger's courtroom persona can easily fool the casual observer, who invariably first focuses on his methodical and halting rhetorical style. Several times in the early days of trial, courthouse critics cracked that Roger sounded a little like Lawrence Welk with his uh-one and uh-two cadence.

Although initially distracting, Roger's style not only slows down the jury, but forces it to listen closely to what he has to say. In the heavily circumstantial case, what Roger has had to say is almost as important as the evidence presented.

The jurors appeared to be listening closely Monday as he gave the prosecution's closing argument. Roger went a long way toward making a farce out of the defense theory that Binion probably committed suicide. And he did so without raising his voice more than a few times.

Roger resembles a legal lion only when sitting next to his equally understated co-counsel David Wall. Between them they haven't been good for a single laugh during the six-week trial, but then murder, kidnapping, and robbery are not laughing matters. ...

—John L. Smith
Las Vegas Review-Journal

LAS VEGAS
REVIEW-JOURNAL   LAS VEGAS SUN

SATURDAY

50¢
COMBINED
EDITIONS

May 20, 2000 ★ ·   Final Edition

BINION VERDICT

GUILTY ALL COUNTS

Rick Tabish bows his head as he and Sandy Murphy listen as their verdicts are read. Both were found guilty of murder and other charges in the September 1998 death of Ted Binion, a former gaming executive who was addicted to heroin.

Jeff Scheid/Review-Journal

Murphy, Tabish stoic in defeat

☐ Two defendants in the Binion trial are silent as verdicts that may put them in prison for life are read.

By Peter O'Connell
Review-Journal

Amid the tears and cheers that greeted the jury's verdict in the Ted Binion murder trial late Friday afternoon, Rick Tabish and Sandy Murphy were the calm at the center of the storm.

Hoots of approval from the overflow crowd monitoring the proceedings on television down the hall wafted into the courtroom as the foreman announced the first of 17 guilty verdicts.

Binion's sister Becky Behnen, tears welling in her eyes, stared blankly at the floor. Tabish's mother, Lani, wept and bore the expression of one who has just lost a son.

Four of the nine women on the jury watched the proceedings through sunglasses that they wore to court with the permission of the judge.

But as they heard the verdicts that will keep them in prison for at least 20 years, Tabish and Murphy limited their reactions to a shake of the head and a downward glance. Twice, Tabish reached over and touched his lover's arm.

The stoicism was especially striking for the 28-year-old Murphy, whose emotional displays have become a fixture of court proceedings.

"This young lady is strong, and she is going to continue to fight until she is vindicated," Murphy attorney John Momot said outside court.

Behnen, who publicly and privately beseeched authorities to treat her brother's death as a homicide when all signs pointed to a drug overdose, derived her own vindication from the verdict.

As she sipped a margarita at Binion's Horseshoe, the downtown casino she controls, Behnen said she knew what her brother would say about the jury's decision.

"He'd be saying, 'The bitch got what she deserved, and she's the most evil, devious, deceptive person I've ever met,'" Behnen said.

The verdict was a rout for the prosecution, with jurors convicting the two defendants on all charges.

Please see BINION/2A

Becky Behnen, Ted Binion's sister, rests her head on the shoulder of her husband, Nick. Their son, Benny, looks back and waits for the verdicts.

THE STATE
OF NEVADA
VS.
SANDRA
RENEE
MURPHY

☑ GUILTY of murder in the first degree

☑ GUILTY of robbery

☑ GUILTY of burglary

☑ GUILTY of grand larceny

☑ GUILTY of two counts of conspiracy

THE STATE
OF NEVADA
VS.
RICHARD
BENNETT
TABISH

☑ GUILTY of murder in the first degree

☑ GUILTY of false imprisonment with use of a deadly weapon

☑ GUILTY of extortion with use of a deadly weapon

☑ GUILTY of assault with use of a deadly weapon

☑ GUILTY of burglary, grand larceny, robbery, and four counts of conspiracy

VERDICT SCENE/PAGE 4A
BY THE NUMBERS/PAGE 4A
SISTER VINDICATED/PAGE 5A
ONLINE REACTION/PAGE 5A

TED BINION

Except for the Sun pages, this combined newspaper was written, edited and designed by the Las Vegas Review-Journal. The Review-Journal published the combined edition for both newspapers under a joint operating agreement. The Las Vegas Sun portions of this combined publication are protected by Copyright (1999) Las Vegas Sun Inc.

Review-Journal   combined Sun
Vol. 96, No. 30   Vol. 50, No. 324
112 total pages

♲

5 65511 00001

Verdict at Horseshoe: Justice was served

☐ People at a casino that was home to Ted Binion rejoice when a jury rules two defendants are guilty.

By Glenn Puit
Review-Journal

Somewhere, somehow, Ted Binion is having trouble wiping the smile off his face.

This according to those who worked at Binion's Horseshoe during Binion's prime, who enjoyed watching Sandy Murphy and Rick Tabish's downfall on the television screens of the casino's sports book Friday afternoon as the two were found guilty of murder by a Clark County jury.

"I think he (Ted) is saying, 'You little witch,'" said Sherri Stearn, a change-person at the casino who worked briefly with Binion. "He's saying, 'You tried to do me in, but look at this.'"

Frank Thompson, a longtime Horseshoe dice pit box man, said his friend of 20 years is likely celebrating — wherever he is.

"Now Ted can rest in peace," Thompson said. "It shows there is justice in this nation and in this world, because Ted was a good man."

Thompson and Stearn were just two of the hundred or so people who gathered in the downtown casino to soak in the verdicts in the legendary gambling hall where Ted Binion once roamed.

Please see HORSESHOE/6A

As the first verdict for Sandy Murphy is read Friday, Shirley Williams, left, shares a moment of surprise with her sister, Joyce Cataline, in the Binion's Horseshoe sports book. The pair from Michigan followed the trial on Court TV. Between them is Frank Thompson, a longtime Binion employee.

John Gurzinski/Review-Journal

The Verdict
and Aftermath

May 2000—

The reading of the verdict is the most high-profile segment of a trial. If the verdict is guilty, the case enters the penalty phase, in which jurors determine the defendants' sentences. In the Binion case, jurors were asked to decide whether the defendants would receive life with or without the possibility of parole. After sentencing, motions are filed to begin the appeal process.

On Friday, May 19, the jury in the Ted Binion murder case brought in its verdict. As the news that the jury was returning reverberated throughout Southern Nevada, broadcasts were interrupted on all major radio and television stations; even the casinos switched their TV sets to the coverage. Eerily mimicking the nation's fascination with the O.J. Simpson verdict, Las Vegans stopped whatever they were doing to learn the result.

At table from left: John Momot, Sandy Murphy, Rick Tabish, Louis Palazzo, Rob Murdock, Linda Norvell.

Sandy Murphy and Rick Tabish stood stunned while the verdicts were read: Guilty on all counts.

In a bizarre role reversal, an emotional Tabish reached out and squeezed Murphy's arm. Her complete non-response became one of the trial's most discussed moments.

Becky Behnen cried tears of relief on husband Nick's shoulder; their son, Benny, sits in the foreground.

William Fuller, foreground, and Frank and Lani Tabish called the verdict an injustice.

While complete acquittal seemed unlikely, most, such as these spectators at the Horseshoe, did not expect across-the-board convictions.

Even media members, who viewed the verdict from the lawn outside the courthouse, appeared surprised.

As the defendants and their defense team filed out of the courtroom, the disappointment was etched on their faces. The verdicts spoiled the post-trial plans of the defense, who had a big victory party scheduled. Murphy had dinner reservations at Piero's; Tabish's were for Delmonico's. That night, both restaurants received numerous prank phone calls cancelling both reservations. Instead of osso bucco and steak, the defendants ate beef stew, white bread with margarine, and a slice of yellow-frosted cake.

Becky Behnen is swarmed by reporters while leaving the courthouse.

I feel very good that I stuck with my convictions.

—Becky Behnen

Private investigator key to outcome

Tom Dillard emerged from District Court Friday afternoon riding the biggest victory of his investigative career. For the first time in a long time, he managed a smile.

He'd not only won a long series of steak dinner bets with friends and associates who failed to believe a jury would convict Rick Tabish and Sandy Murphy of murder in the death of Ted Binion, but he had finally closed what will go down as perhaps the biggest murder case in Las Vegas history.

… Dillard turned over his interviews to Metro homicide. He lauded the efforts of his associates, Bob Leonard, Jack Holder, and Phil Needham, as well as those of Metro Det. James Buczek.

My plan from the beginning was never to be a state witness in the case, Dillard said.

Obviously, the plan worked. Murphy and Tabish face life in prison. Two defense attorneys are second-guessing their strategy. While Tom Dillard has won the case of a lifetime. …

—John L. Smith
Las Vegas Review-Journal

From left Doris Kilmer Binion, Jack Binion, and Brenda Binion Michaels settle in for the penalty phase.

The weight of the penalty phase of the trial, especially the testimony of his mother, briefly overcame Tabish. In contrast to her actions four days earlier, Murphy attempted to console him.

Tabish's mother, Lani, broke down on the witness stand as she described her son's earlier life as contractor, husband, and father of two young children.

Mary Jo Tabish set aside the reality of her husband's affair and spoke about his attributes as a father. She pleaded for jurors to allow Tabish the possibility of parole. Her testimony, some court observers believed, helped sway the jury to be lenient on the two-time convicted felon. Not long after the trial, however, she filed for divorce and put their Montana home up for sale.

This weapon, presented by the prosecution, showed a different side of Sandy-as-victim. It was allegedly flashed by Murphy during a fight with the man she called her "Teddy Ruxpin."

Stepmother Sandra discussed her daughter's young life, which she claimed included twice being the victim of rape.

Sandy Murphy bows her head while her father Ken assists his wife Sandra after testifiying.

Murphy gave an unsworn statement to the court in which she read a hand-written declaration of her love for Ted Binion. Although she was not allowed to discuss her guilt or innocence, she came precariously close to violating the court's order. Her tears did not appear to impress Judge Bonaventure.

After her statement, a calmed Murphy adjusts John Momot's tie. She was later overheard assuring her stepmother, "I'll be out in nine months. I'm going to be a lean mean machine."

Rick Tabish's unsworn statement appeared decidedly less heartfelt. A gaunt Tabish had dropped from 220 lbs. at the beginning of trial, to 175 at its conclusion.

Both Sandy Murphy and Rick Tabish were sentenced to life with the possibility of parole. Jack Binion, right, pictured with attorney Steve Stein, was obviously not displeased with the verdict.

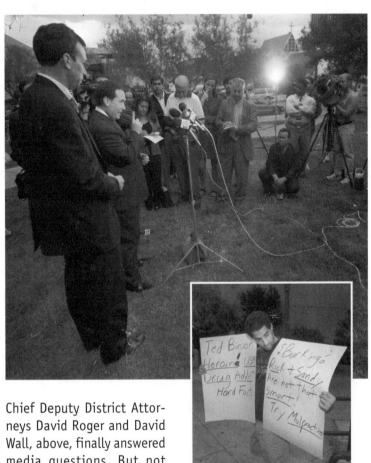

Chief Deputy District Attorneys David Roger and David Wall, above, finally answered media questions. But not everyone was convinced of the defendants' guilt of crimes ranging from murder to grand larceny.

After sentencing, jury foreman Arthur Spear, bottom, was criticized for distributing a timeline to his fellow jurors that included the phrase "depraved indifference." Juror, Joan Sanders, top, later filed an affidavit saying that the term influenced her vote to convict, and that she no longer believed the defendants were guilty. Although five jurors said they had heard the term "depraved indifference"—a legal term not part of the jury instructions—used during deliberations Bonaventure said it did not constitute a violation of the defendants' rights and denied a defense motion to throw out the case on those grounds.

Juror Elmer Glazener admitted he used a Palm Pilot during deliberations to write a check, access a list of toll-free airline telephone numbers, and to perform a math calculation. He denied he used the device to access the Internet, and Judge Bonaventure denied the defense's claim that its presence prejudiced the jury.

Attorneys worked to win the defendants a retrial on several grounds, none of which persuaded Judge Bonaventure. For the convicted couple, reality was sinking in.

On September 15, 2000, nearly two years to the day of Binion's murder, additional prison time accompanied the convictions related to the Pahrump silver theft and the extortion and kidnapping of Leo Casey. Tabish's final admonishment of the prosecution sounded like the words of a con man whose patter had finally stopped working.

Kenneth Murphy, upper left, became so disgusted that he lashed out at the verdict before leaving court. Frank and Lani Tabish, below, had experienced a parent's worst nightmare.

Binion's Pahrump ranch at 700 E. Wilson Road was the scene of a treasure hunt following the sentencing of Murphy and Tabish. Former Binion ranch foreman David Mattsen, bottom, promised he'd be able to find some of Binion's fortune, but the move, which was an attempt to help reduce his criminal culpability, found nothing of substance. Prosecutor David Roger, center (right), had agreed to the excursion against his better judgement.

"Finito," Judge Joseph Bonaventure announced, calling to a close Southern Nevada's first made-for-television murder case. Afterward, the judge would be rumored to be under consideration for a "People's Court"-style TV courtroom show of his own.

Appendix

QUICKSILVER

Quotes from the Case

The Ted Binion murder trial brought together many of Las Vegas' most colorful characters, and their quotes appear throughout the text of this book. Several of the best comments that do not appear in the text—spoken at trial, to reporters, and personally conveyed to the authors—are presented below.

Twenty-five seconds after I met him [Tabish] I told him [Ted] that this son-of-a-bitch is going to rob you.
—Ted Binion's nephew, Bobby Fechser

You can tell a good horse from a bad horse by looking in his eyes.
—Bobby Fechser, warning Ted Binion about Rick Tabish

She was the root of this entire thing—the greed, the lust. She betrayed my uncle, killed him.
—Bobby Fechser

It was a romance that began the way many romances begin in Las Vegas, in a strip club.
—Playboy Magazine

I'm sitting here rotting. I have a wife and two kids. I have a business. And they're making me look like a shyster, a thief, a gigolo. But this is the kind of stuff that happens in Nevada all the time. Ask anyone.
—Rick Tabish to Playboy Magazine

What a tragedy.
—Rick Tabish, upon arriving at the murder scene

Becky Binion Behnen to Ted Binion: *That's a very dangerous thing, to put somebody in your will.*
Ted to Becky: *Don't worry. I've taken the bullets out of all the guns.*

Rick is not the type of man to run and hide, but rather to meet his opponents head-on and prove himself to the world. I know him better than anyone, and at this time his main concerns are to clear his name, pay his debts, and take care of his family. … Unfortunately, people don't realize that the press is putting a spin on reality to influence their thinking and creating a mini-drama to keep them coming back for more. … For the press, the ultimate end to this story would be "guilty." Rick doesn't deserve to be part of this media charade. … I won't be able to hold onto what little is left without him, for the vultures are circling, and with every day he spends incarcerated, they loom ever closer.

—Mary Jo Tabish, in a letter to the court

Ted Binion spent an estimated $1 million on his heroin habit in his lifetime.

—Trial testimony

He could have $1 million at any given time there. He liked to deal in cash.

—Doris Kilmer Binion, addressing the absence of money in the Palomino Lane house

Ted wasn't the kind to be depressed. He was the last guy in the world who would kill himself.

—Binion friend Jay Kerr, who spoke to Binion the day before he died

APPENDIX

Murphy [has never] met a microphone she didn't like.
—Norm Clarke

They were sad.
—Gardener Tom Loveday, referring to Ted Binion's
two dogs on the day of the murder

Murphy to Binion: *Every woman needs a beating once a
month, ain't that right, babe?*
Binion to Murphy: *Yeah, and you got yours already.*
—Conversation related by Barbara Brown

*I cannot allow that, Mr. Palazzo, for you to beat your
client about the head and face with a phone book.*
—District Judge Joseph Bonaventure

*I hope you're happy. This town ought to be ashamed of
themselves for what they did to our son.*
—Frank Tabish, after the trial, to David Roger,
Tom Dillard, and Bobby Fechser

*[Letters have] run the gamut from the ridiculous to the
sublime ... [females] calling up asking if we could send
them autographed pictures ... if the judge is married, if
I'm married.*
—Judge Bonaventure's aide, Al Lasso

*Ted Binion was murdered. He was murdered for lust, he
was murdered for greed. He was murdered by someone he
trusted and her new companion.*
—Chief Deputy District Attorney David Roger

QUICKSILVER

They would have given anything to be part of the Binion money. They wanted it and each other enough to kill an eccentric, wealthy heroin addict.
—Chief Deputy District Attorney David Wall

Coincidence of coincidences, he committed suicide on the day someone emptied all the valuables out of his safe.
—David Wall

There may not be anything like it until the next trial of the century.
—David Wall

The Unsworn Statement of Sandra Renee Murphy
— May 24, 2000 —

Hi, my name is Sandy Murphy, and I know you haven't had a chance to hear from me yet. But I've been very anxious to share the truth—the truth about what happened to Teddy. Regretfully, I did not testify, but now I can see that was a mistake. But instead of looking at what could have been, I can only look at what will be.

So this will be the first and final time we get to know each other. I respect and sympathize with each and every one of you for the awesome task you have before you. As I look about the room today I see pain and suffering all around me: Bonnie for the loss of her father; Becky, Brenda and Jeff for the loss of their brother; the Fechsers and all the family and friends that were touched by Teddy's life. For the Tabish family, who have also suffered the loss of a son, a husband, a brother and an uncle, and for Amanda and Kyle for the loss of their father.

For my family, for my parents and my brothers and sisters. (Inaudible) niece and a godmother, and for Tony and Ryan and the loss of their Auntie Sandy.

For my friend, Rick Tabish, who whenever I called was always there, who stoodby my side when no one did and who believed in me and was always there to lend a helping hand or an ear to listen to. For the life that he's lost and the one that will never come.

For my loss, for the loss of my Teddy "Ruxpin." He was the man that swept me off my feet. I thought he was my fix-it man. I thought he would fill the hole in my heart. I thought he would always love and protect me. He bought me a wedding band, and the inscription read: "With undying love, Teddy." I miss the early mornings when he would wake me up to watch the sunrise, to play ball with Princess and take (inaudible) and see the birds in the morning. The first thing that Teddy taught me was how to ride horses. We used to go to the farm in Pahrump and ride at sundown. We would watch countless hours of History, A & E, and Discovery Channel. He was like a sponge for knowledge. I miss the flowers that we would plant in the garden together on special days, all the romantic nights in front of the fireplace in our bedroom. I miss the talks on our bench under the tree that made heart-shaped leaves. Teddy was the kind of guy that had this smile, and no matter what he did or how angry you were at him, all he had to do was bat his eyes and smile. He always had me right where he wanted me. But most of all I miss his face, I miss his voice, and I miss his touch.

I have loved and lost, but I have learned to just take the good memories and go on. I know you heard some ugly things about Teddy during these proceedings, but that was Teddy the heroin addict. There are trials and tribulations in every relationship, and sometimes we get lost and go astray, but that doesn't mean that we love each other any less. I love Teddy with all my heart, and I know he loves me just as much. You may have taken away my freedom, but no matter what goes on in these proceedings, or what anybody ever says about us, you can never take a way the love we had for each other.

I am so sad for all my hopes and dreams, for the family I will never have, the wedding that will never be, and my children that will never come.

Last night I lay in bed thinking of what I wanted to say here today, and there was one thing that stuck out in my mind. There was something that I need to do for me. I want to say that I'm sorry to the Binion family, but most of all I'm sorry to Bonnie, and I'm sorry for the day I walked out that door on September 17th and left him there alone. And I'm sorry to Teddy for not being there when he needed me the most. And I'm sorry. ... Thank you.

The Unsworn Statement of Richard Bennett Tabish
— May 24, 2000 —

It's hard. It's hard on everybody. There's been so many things that needed to come out, and I just can't talk.

My heart's out to the Binion family, I mean that sincerely. I can look everybody in that front row in the eye and tell you I am sorry. And please take that from my heart because that's where it's coming from.

I hope someday something can get rectified. The prosecution did their job. They put on a case. I'm not supposed to talk about the case so I won't go there. ... I know you guys (the jury) had a big burden, and you did what you had to do based on the evidence presented to you, and I applaud you.

Let's talk about who Rick Tabish is. Twenty months have gone by. There's been a lot about Rick Tabish. Let me tell you who I am. I'm proud of who I am. ... I was an overachiever. I should have listened to my father. He told me all the time, 'Learn how to walk before you run, Rick.' I never listened. I should have listened to my father. I wouldn't be sitting here today.

Old school has ruined me, because a handshake and loyalty doesn't work anymore. It hasn't worked for me. Every time I've been in trouble. ... I've had trouble associating with my generation because they don't have old-school values. Hit hard, run fast. I'm not about that.

I'm not perfect by all means. I'm not standing here saying I'm perfect. I've made my mistakes. I've made my mistakes in this situation. ... I have no real regrets about anything I did except getting involved in this situation. My heart's broke because everybody else is destroyed. If I could go spend the rest of my life in prison, or if I could give my life so that my mother, my two brothers that sat up here crying, could live their lives without knowing that their brother is going to prison for the rest of his, I would do it. I'm not that selfish of a man.

For every time I held my head up, for every time I smiled in this court, for every time I smiled for a news camera, for every bit of cocky attitude I had during this case, I'm ashamed of myself. I'm disgusted.

I had the attitude nothing was good enough, and when the verdict came back, it was good enough. Everybody's worked for me. I've taken advantage of everybody's hard work. And I'm sorry, but in return what I have to say is I'm proud of who I am. You guys have returned a verdict on me, that's your decision. I'm going to live with that decision. I'm man enough to live with that decision.

Some of the greatest lessons in life are hardship. ... You don't learn until your hands are slapped.

The Sentences

The sentencing was one of the most complicated aspects of the Binion trial. At one point after sentences were announced, people compared notes in the hallway outside the courtroom, trying to ascertain who was doing time for what. The exact sentences for each of the principals are outlined below.

Sandy Murphy

Sandra Renee Murphy received a sentence of 22 years-to life. First parole eligibility: 2021.

Count I .... Conspiracy to Commit Robbery: 28-72 months

Count VII ...... Murder: life with the possibility of parole, eligible for parole after 20 years

Count VIII .... Robbery: 72-180 months, concurrently with Count VII

Count IX .... Conspiracy to Commit Burglary: 12 months, concurrently with Count VII

Count X .... Burglary: 24-120 months, consecutively with Count VII

Count XI .... Grand Larceny: 48-120 months, concurrently with Count IX

Credit for time served 213 days.

Rick Tabish

Richard Bennett Tabish received a sentence of 25 years-to-life.
First parole eligibility: 2024
$10,992 restitution to Clark County
$7,000 restitution to Leo Casey

Count I .... Conspiracy to Commit Robbery: 28-72 months

Count II .... Conspiracy to Commit Extortion: 28-72 months, concurrently

Count III .... Conspiracy to Commit Kidnapping: dismissed

Count IV .... False Imprisonment: 28-72 months, concurrently

Count V .... Assault with Deadly Weapon: 28-72 months, concurrently

Count VI .... Extortion, with Deadly Weapon: 18-120 months, consecutively with Count V

Count VII ...... Murder: life with the possibility of parole

Count VIII .... Robbery: 72-180 months, concurrently with Count VII

Count IX .... Conspiracy to Commit Burglary: 12 months concurrent with CountVII

Count X .... Burglary: 24-120 months, consecutively with Count VII

Count XI .... Grand Larceny: 48-120 months concurrently with Count IX

Credit for time served 451 days.

The Pahrump Silver Heist

David Mattsen pled no contest to conspiracy to commit grand larceny and was sentenced to a $2,000 fine or 200 hours of community service. He served the hours.

Michael Milot pled no contest to conspiracy to commit grand larceny, paid a $2,000 fine, and was given credit for time served.

The Leo Casey Extortion

Steven Wadkins pled no contest to conspiracy to commit extortion, paid a $2,000 fine, and forfeited his gun and concealed weapons permit.

John Joseph pled no contest to conspiracy to commit extortion, paid a $2,000 fine, and forfeited his concealed-weapons permit.

Timeline for September 17, 1998
Source: Private investigator Tom Dillard

4 a.m.—Sierra Health Services Chief Engineer Willis John Reiker arrives at work at 888 S. Rancho Road and is met by his friend Lonnie Ted Binion.

5 a.m.—7-Eleven clerk Marvin Reed greets regular customer Binion at the store located at the corner of Charleston Boulevard and Rancho Road.

5:30 a.m.—Housekeeper Eunice Altamirano, who resides at the home of Dr. Enrique Lacayo at 2400 Palomino Lane, greets Binion and hands him the morning *Review-Journal*.

9 a.m.—Gardener Thomas Loveday arrives at 2408 Palomino Lane for his weekly maintenance of Binion's yard. He remains at the residence until 1 p.m. and sees no one leave the house, but notes that the family dogs anxiously scratched at the sliding-glass door in the rear of the residence.

9 a.m.—Housekeeper Mary Montoya-Gasciogne receives a call at her home from Sandy Murphy instructing her not to come to work.

12:15 p.m.—Real-estate-agent Barbara Brown calls the Palomino Lane house to speak with Binion and is told by Murphy that "he's out." Brown's appointment with Binion, which was made at 9 p.m. the previous day, is abruptly canceled.

3 p.m.—Horseshoe Gaming Executive Assistant Cathy Rose is interrupted during a meeting by Sandy Murphy, who is present at the office at 4024 Industrial Road to present a check for a small amount of money.

3:15 p.m.—Rose receives a call from Murphy asking for a

phone number for an Alaskan fishing guide who had befriended Binion.

3:16 p.m.—Records show an outgoing call made from Rick Tabish's cell phone to Horseshoe Gaming, meaning Murphy used Tabish's phone to call Rose.

3:47 p.m.—Murphy receives a call on her cell phone from Rick Tabish's cell phone.

3:55 p.m.—Murphy reports finding Binion's body at the Palomino Lane house and dials 9-1-1.

The Criminal Complaint

THE STATE OF NEVADA,	)
Plaintiff,	) CASE NO. 99F08732A-F
-vs-	)
Richard Bennett Tabish,	)
#	)
John Bradford Joseph,	)
#	)
Steven Lee Wadkins,	) CRIMINAL COMPLAINT
#0647239	)
Sandra Renee Murphy,	)
#	)
Michael David Milot,	)
#	)
David Lee Mattsen,	)
aka David Eugene Gaeth,	)
#0452470	)
Defendants.	)

The Defendants above named have committed the crimes of **CONSPIRACY TO COMMIT MURDER AND/OR ROBBERY (Felony - NRS 199.480, 200.010, 200.030, 200.380); CONSPIRACY TO COMMIT EXTORTION (Gross Misdemeanor - NRS 199.480, 205.320); CONSPIRACY TO COMMIT KIDNAPPING (Felony - NRS 199.480, 200.320); ASSAULT WITH A DEADLY WEAPON (Felony - NRS 200.471); FIRST DEGREE KIDNAPPING WITH USE OF A DEADLY WEAPON (Felony - NRS 200.320, 193.165); EXTORTION WITH USE OF A DEADLY WEAPON (Felony - NRS 205.320, 193.165); MURDER WITH USE OF A DEADLY WEAPON (OPEN) (Felony - NRS 200.010, 200.030, 193.165); ROBBERY WITH USE OF A DEADLY WEAPON (Felony - NRS 200.380, 193.165); CONSPIRACY TO COMMIT BURGLARY AND/OR GRAND LARCENY (Felony - NRS 199.480, 205.060, 205.220); BURGLARY (Felony - NRS 205.060); and GRAND LARCENY (Felony - NRS 205.220)**, in the manner following, to-wit:

///

APPENDIX

1   That the said Defendant(s), on or between April, 1998, and September 19, 1998, and committed

2   the following offenses within the County of Clark, State of Nevada, and/or committed acts or

3   effects thereof in the County of Clark, State of Nevada constituting or requisite to the

4   consummation of offenses occurring in the County of Nye, State of Nevada,

5   COUNT I - CONSPIRACY TO COMMIT MURDER AND/OR ROBBERY

6   Defendants RICHARD BENNETT TABISH and SANDRA RENEE MURPHY did,

7   between April, 1998, and September 19, 1998, then and there meet with others and between

8   themselves, and each of them with the other, wilfully and unlawfully conspire and agree to

9   commit the crime of Murder and/or Robbery, and in furtherance of said Conspiracy, Defendants

10   did commit the acts as set forth in Counts VII through VIII, said acts being incorporated by this

11   reference as set forth herein.

12   COUNT II - CONSPIRACY TO COMMIT EXTORTION

13   Defendants RICHARD BENNETT TABISH, JOHN BRADFORD JOSEPH, and

14   STEVEN LEE WADKINS, did, between July 25, 1998, and July 28, 1998, then and there meet

15   with others and between themselves, and each of them with the other, wilfully and unlawfully

16   conspire and agree to commit the crime of Extortion, and in furtherance of said Conspiracy,

17   Defendants did commit the acts as set forth in Counts III - VI, said acts being incorporated by

18   this reference as set forth herein.

19   COUNT III - CONSPIRACY TO COMMIT KIDNAPPING

20   Defendants RICHARD BENNETT TABISH, JOHN BRADFORD JOSEPH and

21   STEVEN LEE WADKINS, did, between July 25, 1998, and July 28, 1998, then and there meet

22   with others and between themselves, and each of them with the other, wilfully and unlawfully

23   conspire and agree to commit the crime of Kidnapping, and in furtherance of said Conspiracy,

24   Defendants did commit the acts as set forth in Counts II, IV - VI, said acts being incorporated

25   by this reference as set forth herein.

26   COUNT IV - FIRST DEGREE KIDNAPPING WITH USE OF A DEADLY WEAPON

27   Defendants RICHARD BENNETT TABISH, JOHN BRADFORD JOSEPH and

28   STEVEN LEE WADKINS, did, on or about July 28, 1998, wilfully, unlawfully, feloniously,

-2-

189

1 and without authority of law, seize, confine, inveigle, entice, decoy, abduct, conceal, kidnap,
2 or carry away LEO CASEY, a human being, with the intent to hold or detain the said LEO
3 CASEY against his will and without his consent, for the purpose of committing Extortion, said
4 Defendants using a deadly weapon, to-wit: a firearm, during the commission of said crime;
5 Defendants RICHARD BENNETT TABISH, JOHN BRADFORD JOSEPH and STEVEN LEE
6 WADKINS aiding or abetting each other by acting in concert; and/or Defendants RICHARD
7 BENNETT TABISH, JOHN BRADFORD JOSEPH and STEVEN LEE WADKINS counseling
8 and encouraging each other by Defendant JOHN BRADFORD JOSEPH persuading LEO
9 CASEY to go with Defendants RICHARD BENNETT TABISH and STEVEN LEE WADKINS
10 to a desert area under the pretext of Defendants RICHARD BENNETT TABISH and STEVEN
11 LEE WADKINS examining equipment that Defendant JOHN BRADFORD JOSEPH allegedly
12 desired to sell, Defendants RICHARD BENNETT TABISH and STEVEN LEE WADKINS
13 restraining LEO CASEY with thumb-cuffs upon arriving at the desert area, Defendant STEVEN
14 LEE WADKINS forcing a firearm into the mouth of LEO CASEY and threatening to kill LEO
15 CASEY, Defendant RICHARD BENNETT TABISH repeatedly striking LEO CASEY about the
16 head and body with a telephone book, Defendant RICHARD BENNETT TABISH directing
17 Defendant STEVEN LEE WADKINS to dig a potential grave for LEO CASEY, both Defendants
18 RICHARD BENNETT TABISH and STEVEN LEE WADKINS forcing LEO CASEY to walk
19 to the edge of the excavated grave at which time LEO CASEY relented and agreed to the
20 demands of Defendants JOHN BRADFORD JOSEPH, RICHARD BENNETT TABISH and
21 STEVEN LEE WADKINS; and/or Defendants JOHN BRADFORD JOSEPH, RICHARD
22 BENNETT TABISH and STEVEN LEE WADKINS transporting LEO CASEY, still restrained
23 by thumb-cuffs, to a law office for the purpose of signing a confession and asset transfer
24 agreement, Defendant STEVEN LEE WADKINS aiming a firearm at the head and body of LEO
25 CASEY during the trip to the law offices; and/or Defendants RICHARD BENNETT TABISH,
26 JOHN BRADFORD JOSEPH and STEVEN LEE WADKINS acting pursuant to a Conspiracy
27 to Commit Kidnapping and Extortion.
28 ///

-3-

190

APPENDIX

1 | <u>COUNT V</u> - ASSAULT WITH A DEADLY WEAPON

2 | Defendants RICHARD BENNETT TABISH, JOHN BRADFORD JOSEPH and

3 | STEVEN LEE WADKINS, did, on or about July 28, 1998, coupled with the present ability,

4 | wilfully, unlawfully, and feloniously attempt to commit a violent injury, with use of a deadly

5 | weapon, upon the person of another, to-wit: LEO CASEY by forcing a firearm into the mouth

6 | of LEO CASEY and threatening to kill LEO CASEY, with a firearm; Defendant STEVEN LEE

7 | WADKINS directly committing said acts and Defendants JOHN BRADFORD JOSEPH and

8 | RICHARD BENNETT TABISH aiding or abetting Defendant STEVEN LEE WADKINS in the

9 | commission of said acts by all Defendants acting in concert; and/or Defendants RICHARD

10 | BENNETT TABISH, JOHN BRADFORD JOSEPH and STEVEN LEE WADKINS counseling

11 | and encouraging each other by Defendant JOHN BRADFORD JOSEPH persuading LEO

12 | CASEY to go with Defendants RICHARD BENNETT TABISH and STEVEN LEE WADKINS

13 | to a desert area under the pretext of Defendants RICHARD BENNETT TABISH and STEVEN

14 | LEE WADKINS examining equipment that Defendant JOHN BRADFORD JOSEPH allegedly

15 | desired to sell, Defendants RICHARD BENNETT TABISH and STEVEN LEE WADKINS

16 | restraining LEO CASEY with thumb-cuffs upon arriving at the desert area, Defendant STEVEN

17 | LEE WADKINS forcing a firearm into the mouth of LEO CASEY and threatening to kill LEO

18 | CASEY, Defendant RICHARD BENNETT TABISH repeatedly striking LEO CASEY about the

19 | head and body with a telephone book, Defendant RICHARD BENNETT TABISH directing

20 | Defendant STEVEN LEE WADKINS to dig a potential grave for LEO CASEY, both Defendants

21 | RICHARD BENNETT TABISH and STEVEN LEE WADKINS forcing LEO CASEY to walk

22 | to the edge of the excavated grave at which time LEO CASEY relented and agreed to the

23 | demands of Defendants JOHN BRADFORD JOSEPH, RICHARD BENNETT TABISH and

24 | STEVEN LEE WADKINS; and/or Defendants JOHN BRADFORD JOSEPH, RICHARD

25 | BENNETT TABISH and STEVEN LEE WADKINS transporting LEO CASEY, still restrained

26 | by thumb-cuffs, to a law office for the purpose of signing a confession and asset transfer

27 | agreement, Defendant STEVEN LEE WADKINS aiming a firearm at the head and body of LEO

28 | CASEY during the trip to the law offices; and/or Defendants RICHARD BENNETT TABISH,

-4-

1　JOHN BRADFORD JOSEPH and STEVEN LEE WADKINS acting pursuant to a Conspiracy

2　to Commit Kidnapping and Extortion.

3　COUNT VI - EXTORTION WITH USE OF A DEADLY WEAPON

4　　　Defendants RICHARD BENNETT TABISH, JOHN BRADFORD JOSEPH and

5　STEVEN LEE WADKINS, did, on or about July 28, 1998, then and there wilfully, unlawfully,

6　and feloniously threaten to injure LEO CASEY and/or threaten to accuse LEO CASEY of the

7　crime of Embezzlement with the intent to extort or gain property, to-wit: equipment and/or

8　mining rights and/or with the intent to compel or induce LEO CASEY to execute a writing

9　affecting and intended to affect property, to-wit: a confession and asset transfer agreement, said

10　Defendants using a deadly weapon, to-wit: a firearm, during the commission of said crime; by

11　Defendants RICHARD BENNETT TABISH, JOHN BRADFORD JOSEPH and STEVEN LEE

12　WADKINS aiding or abetting each other by acting in concert; and/or Defendants RICHARD

13　BENNETT TABISH, JOHN BRADFORD JOSEPH and STEVEN LEE WADKINS counseling

14　and encouraging each other by Defendant JOHN BRADFORD JOSEPH persuading LEO

15　CASEY to go with Defendants RICHARD BENNETT TABISH and STEVEN LEE WADKINS

16　to a desert area under the pretext of Defendants RICHARD BENNETT TABISH and STEVEN

17　LEE WADKINS examining equipment that Defendant JOHN BRADFORD JOSEPH allegedly

18　desired to sell, Defendants RICHARD BENNETT TABISH and STEVEN LEE WADKINS

19　restraining LEO CASEY with thumb-cuffs upon arriving at the desert area, Defendant STEVEN

20　LEE WADKINS forcing a firearm into the mouth of LEO CASEY and threatening to kill LEO

21　CASEY, Defendant RICHARD BENNETT TABISH repeatedly striking LEO CASEY about the

22　head and body with a telephone book, Defendant RICHARD BENNETT TABISH directing

23　Defendant STEVEN LEE WADKINS to dig a potential grave for LEO CASEY, both Defendants

24　RICHARD BENNETT TABISH and STEVEN LEE WADKINS forcing LEO CASEY to walk

25　to the edge of the excavated grave at which time LEO CASEY relented and agreed to the

26　demands of Defendants JOHN BRADFORD JOSEPH, RICHARD BENNETT TABISH and

27　STEVEN LEE WADKINS; and/or Defendants JOHN BRADFORD JOSEPH, RICHARD

28　BENNETT TABISH and STEVEN LEE WADKINS transporting LEO CASEY, still restrained

-5-

192

1   by thumb-cuffs, to a law office for the purpose of signing a confession and asset transfer

2   agreement, Defendant STEVEN LEE WADKINS aiming a firearm at the head and body of LEO

3   CASEY during the trip to the law offices; and/or Defendants RICHARD BENNETT TABISH,

4   JOHN BRADFORD JOSEPH and STEVEN LEE WADKINS acting pursuant to a Conspiracy

5   to Commit Kidnapping and Extortion.

6   <u>COUNT VII</u> - MURDER WITH USE OF A DEADLY WEAPON (OPEN)

7   Defendants RICHARD BENNETT TABISH and SANDRA RENEE MURPHY did, on

8   or about September 17, 1998, then and there, without authority of law, with malice aforethought

9   and premeditation and/or during the perpetration or attempted perpetration of Burglary and/or

10   Robbery, wilfully and feloniously kill LONNIE TED BINION, a human being, by means of

11   subterfuge or force, cause LONNIE TED BINION to ingest lethal doses of Xanax and Heroin,

12   said Defendants using a deadly weapon, to-wit: Xanax and/or Heroin, during the commission

13   of said crime, Defendants RICHARD BENNETT TABISH and SANDRA RENEE MURPHY

14   directly committing said acts; and/or Defendants RICHARD BENNETT TABISH and SANDRA

15   RENEE MURPHY aiding or abetting each other in the commission of said acts by acting in

16   concert with each other; and/or Defendants RICHARD BENNETT TABISH and SANDRA

17   RENEE MURPHY being present before, during and after said acts; and/or Defendants

18   RICHARD BENNETT TABISH and SANDRA RENEE MURPHY directly or indirectly

19   counseling, encouraging, assisting, commanding, inducing or supervising the actions of the

20   other; and/or Defendants RICHARD BENNETT TABISH and SANDRA RENEE MURPHY

21   acting pursuant to a Conspiracy to Commit Murder and/or Robbery.

22   <u>COUNT VIII</u> - ROBBERY WITH USE OF A DEADLY WEAPON

23   Defendants RICHARD BENNETT TABISH and SANDRA RENEE MURPHY did,

24   between September 17, 1998, and September 19, 1998, then and there wilfully, unlawfully and

25   feloniously take personal property, to-wit: United States currency and/or coin collections and/or

26   silver coins and bars, from the person of LONNIE TED BINION, or in his presence, by means

27   of force or violence, or fear of injury to, and without the consent and against the will of the said

28   LONNIE TED BINION; said Defendants using a deadly weapon, to-wit: Xanax and/or Heroin,

1 during the commission of said crime; Defendants RICHARD BENNETT TABISH and

2 SANDRA RENEE MURPHY aiding or abetting each other in the commission of said acts by

3 acting in concert with each other; and/or Defendants RICHARD BENNETT TABISH and

4 SANDRA RENEE MURPHY being present before, during and after said acts; and/or

5 DEFENDANTS RICHARD BENNETT TABISH and SANDRA RENEE MURPHY killing

6 LONNIE TED BINION; and/or Defendants RICHARD BENNETT TABISH and SANDRA

7 RENEE MURPHY directly or indirectly counseling, encouraging, assisting, commanding,

8 inducing or supervising the actions of the other; and/or Defendants RICHARD BENNETT

9 TABISH and SANDRA RENEE MURPHY acting pursuant to a Conspiracy to Commit Murder

10 and/or Robbery.

11 <u>COUNT IX</u> - CONSPIRACY TO COMMIT BURGLARY AND/OR GRAND LARCENY

12   Defendants RICHARD BENNETT TABISH, SANDRA RENEE MURPHY, DAVID

13 LEE MATTSEN, and MICHAEL DAVID MILOT, did, between September 16, 1998, and

14 September 19, 1998, then and there meet with others and between themselves, and each of them

15 with the other, wilfully and unlawfully conspire and agree to commit the crime of Murder and/or

16 Robbery, and in furtherance of said Conspiracy, Defendant did commit the acts as set forth in

17 Counts X and XI, said acts being incorporated by this reference as set forth herein.

18 <u>COUNT X</u> - BURGLARY

19   Defendants RICHARD BENNETT TABISH, SANDRA RENEE MURPHY, DAVID

20 LEE MATTSEN and MICHAEL DAVID MILOT, did, on or between September 18, 1998, and

21 September 19, 1998, then and there wilfully, unlawfully, and feloniously enter, with intent to

22 commit larceny, that certain underground vault, located at a desert area in Pahrump, Nye

23 County, Nevada, the property of LONNIE TED BINION; Defendants RICHARD BENNETT

24 TABISH, SANDRA RENEE MURPHY, DAVID LEE MATTSEN and MICHAEL DAVID

25 MILOT aiding or abetting each other in the commission of said acts by acting in concert with

26 each other; and/or by Defendants RICHARD BENNETT TABISH and SANDRA RENEE

27 MURPHY killing LONNIE TED BINION; and/or Defendants RICHARD BENNETT TABISH,

28 SANDRA RENEE MURPHY, DAVID LEE MATTSEN and MICHAEL DAVID MILOT

-7-

194

APPENDIX

1   directly or indirectly counseling, encouraging, assisting, commanding, inducing or supervising
2   the actions of the other; and/or Defendants RICHARD BENNETT TABISH and MICHAEL
3   DAVID MILOT acquiring equipment to be used in the excavation of the vault and the
4   transportation of the silver; and/or Defendants RICHARD BENNETT TABISH, DAVID LEE
5   MATTSEN and MICHAEL DAVID MILOT excavating the underground vault, removing said
6   silver from the vault and loading the silver into a truck; and/or all Defendants acting pursuant
7   to a Conspiracy to Commit Burglary and/or Grand Larceny.
8   COUNT XI - GRAND LARCENY
9   Defendants RICHARD BENNETT TABISH, SANDRA RENEE MURPHY, DAVID
10 LEE MATTSEN and MICHAEL DAVID MILOT, did, on or between September 18, 1998, and
11 September 19, 1998, then and there wilfully, unlawfully and feloniously, with intent to deprive
12 the owner permanently thereof, steal, take, and carry away personal property of LONNIE TED
13 BINION, having a value of $250.00, or more, to-wit: silver coins and bars; Defendants
14 RICHARD BENNETT TABISH, SANDRA RENEE MURPHY, DAVID LEE MATTSEN and
15 MICHAEL DAVID MILOT aiding or abetting each other in the commission of said acts by
16 acting in concert with each other; and/or by Defendants RICHARD BENNETT TABISH and
17 SANDRA RENEE MURPHY killing LONNIE TED BINION; and/or Defendants RICHARD
18 BENNETT TABISH, SANDRA RENEE MURPHY, DAVID LEE MATTSEN and MICHAEL
19 DAVID MILOT directly or indirectly counseling, encouraging, assisting, commanding, inducing
20 or supervising the actions of the other; and/or Defendants RICHARD BENNETT TABISH and
21 MICHAEL DAVID MILOT acquiring equipment to be used in the excavation of the vault and
22 the transportation of the silver; and/or Defendants RICHARD BENNETT TABISH, DAVID
23 LEE MATTSEN and MICHAEL DAVID MILOT excavating the underground vault, removing
24 said silver from the vault and loading the silver into a truck; and/or all Defendants acting
25 pursuant to a Conspiracy to Commit Burglary and/or Grand Larceny.
26 ///
27 ///
28 ///

-8-

195

QUICKSILVER

1   All of which is contrary to the form, force and effect of Statutes in such cases made and

2 provided and against the peace and dignity of the State of Nevada. Said Complainant makes this

3 declaration subject to the penalty of perjury.

4

5   06/21/99

6

7

8

9

10

11

12

13

14

15

16

17

18

19

20

21

22

23

24 DA#99F08732A-F/kjh
LVMPD EV#9809171397

25 CONSP MURDER/ROBB; CONSP
EXTORTION; CONSP KIDNAP;

26 1° KIDNAP W/WPN; AWDW;
EXTORT W/WPN; MURDER W/WPN;

27 ROBB W/WPN; CONSP BURG &/OR G/L;
BURG; G/L - F

28 (TK)

-9-

APPENDIX

1	JUSTICE COURT, LAS VEGAS TOWNSHIP
2	CLARK COUNTY, NEVADA
3	THE STATE OF NEVADA,
4	Plaintiff, CASE NO. 99F08732A-F
5	-vs-

```
 1          JUSTICE COURT, LAS VEGAS TOWNSHIP
 2              CLARK COUNTY, NEVADA
 3   THE STATE OF NEVADA,
 4              Plaintiff,              )  CASE NO.   99F08732A-F
 5       -vs-                          )
 6   Richard Bennett Tabish,           )
       #                               )
 7   John Bradford Joseph,             )
       #                               )
 8   Steven Lee Wadkins,               )
       #0647239                        )
 9   Sandra Renee Murphy,              )
       #                               )
10   Michael David Milot,              )
       #                               )
11   David Lee Mattsen,                )
       aka David Eugene Gaeth,         )
12     #0452470                        )
13              Defendants.            )
14   _____)
15
16              AFFIDAVIT AND APPLICATION
17              FOR ARREST WARRANTS
18       COMES NOW, the State of Nevada, by STEWART L. BELL, District Attorney, through
19   DAVID J.J. ROGER, Chief Deputy District Attorney, and hereby files the instant Affidavit and
20   Application for Arrest Warrants.
21       DATED this 21ST day of June, 1999.
22                           Respectfully submitted,
23                           STEWART L. BELL
24                           DISTRICT ATTORNEY
                             Nevada Bar #000477
25
26   BY
27                           DAVID J.J. ROGER
                             Chief Deputy District Attorney
28                           Nevada Bar #005043
```

-10-

197

Photo Index

Jeff Scheid, a native of Terry, Montana, located about 150 miles southeast of the Binion Ranch, has worked as a photographer for the *Las Vegas Review-Journal* for the past 20 years. Scheid has covered most major news, entertainment, and sporting events for the newspaper. When not photographing Las Vegas, he and his wife write travel stories for the *Review-Journal* and lasvegas.com

John L. Smith, a fourth-generation Nevadan, is an award-winning columnist for the *Las Vegas Review-Journal* and the author of several acclaimed books, including *No Limit—The Rise and Fall of Bob Stupak and Las Vegas' Stratosphere Tower*. He lives in Las Vegas with his wife and daughter.